**BE
HEALED**

Books by Steve Austin

---

*God Heals*

*Be Healed*

# BE
# HEALED

## A 40-DAY DEVOTIONAL
## TO RECLAIM YOUR HEALTH

## STEVE AUSTIN

**Chosen**
a division of Baker Publishing Group
Minneapolis, Minnesota

© 2024 by Stephen Austin

Published by Chosen Books
Minneapolis, Minnesota
ChosenBooks.com

Chosen Books is a division of
Baker Publishing Group, Grand Rapids, Michigan

Printed in the United States of America

Library of Congress Cataloging-in-Publication Data
Names: Austin, Steve, 1966– author.
Title: Be healed : a 40-day devotional to reclaim your health / Steve Austin.
Description: Minneapolis, Minnesota : Chosen Books, a division of Baker Publishing Group, [2024] | Includes bibliographical references.
Identifiers: LCCN 2023048311 | ISBN 9780800772628 (paper) | ISBN 9780800772635 (casebound) | ISBN 9781493446766 (ebook)
Subjects: LCSH: Spiritual healing. | Healing—Religious aspects—Christianity. | Devotional literature.
Classification: LCC BT732.5 .A95 2024 | DDC 242/.2—dc23/eng/20240126
LC record available at https://lccn.loc.gov/2023048311

This publication is intended to provide helpful and informative material on the subjects addressed. Readers should consult their personal health professionals before adopting any of the suggestions in this book or drawing inferences from it. The author and publisher expressly disclaim responsibility for any adverse effects arising from the use or application of the information contained in this book.

Cover design by Dan Pitts

24  25  26  27  28  29  30        7  6  5  4  3  2  1

# Contents

Introduction   7

Day 1 Anchored in Hope   11

Day 2 God of the Impossible   15

Day 3 All Inclusive   19

Day 4 Just Receive   23

Day 5 Healing Is a Choice   27

Day 6 Fighting from Victory   31

Day 7 Boundless Love   35

Day 8 Your Most Important Identity   41

Day 9 Magnify God over Your Sickness   47

Day 10 Whose Report Will You Believe?   51

Day 11 This Is Only a Test   55

Day 12 Fireproof   59

Day 13 A New Perspective   63

Day 14 The Superpower of Gratitude   67

Day 15 Program Your Mind for Victory   73

Day 16 First See It on the Inside   77

Day 17 Conquering Fear   81

Day 18 The Peace of God   85

Day 19 It Is Well    89

Day 20 Rejoice!    93

Day 21 One Thing Is Needed    99

Day 22 Prayer Power    105

Day 23 Open Your Mouth    109

Day 24 Whatever You Say    113

Day 25 Guard against Negative Words    117

Day 26 Faith over Feelings    121

Day 27 Faith in the Middle    125

Day 28 "I Still Believe" Faith    129

Day 29 Help My Unbelief    135

Day 30 Be a Faith Warrior    139

Day 31 When, God, When?    143

Day 32 Praise Your Way to Victory    147

Day 33 Your Helper    151

Day 34 Heavenly Helpers    155

Day 35 Your Authority in Christ    159

Day 36 How to Use Your Authority in Christ    165

Day 37 Healthy Soul    169

Day 38 Forgiveness    173

Day 39 Serve Somebody    177

Day 40 Body Wise    181

Notes    187

# Introduction

Welcome to this forty-day life-changing journey to reclaim your health! I am going to share with you secrets to healing that I have learned from twenty-five years of ministering to thousands of people in the largest medical center in the world (the Texas Medical Center in Houston, which gets ten million patient visits per year). I have seen countless miraculous healings of virtually every medical condition, and I want to help you receive your own!

Think of me as your healing coach. Great coaches prepare their teams to win, and I want to help you win the battle for your health. The principles I share are not theories or opinions, but they are based on the Word of God, which never fails. I have seen them work for countless people, and I know they will work for you! I have also included many astonishing healing testimonies to encourage your faith. God is no respecter of persons. What He did for others, He will do for you if you believe for it. Jesus said, "If you can believe, *all* things are possible to him who believes" (Mark 9:23).

As the medical professionals do their part, this book will help you do your part to exercise your faith and bring God into the equation. When God is in the mix, anything is possible. He's a God of miracles. Nothing is impossible with Him! He uses doctors and medicine, but He is not limited to that. He can do what doctors and medicine can't do.

God is your Healer. He called Himself *Jehovah Rapha*—"God who heals"—in Exodus 15:26. He connected His very name and identity to healing. Healing is His nature. He healed in Bible times, and He heals today. He never changes. You are His child, and He wants you to be healthy and thriving. He has you in the palm of His hand. He is surrounding what is surrounding you. He is singing songs of deliverance over you (Psalm 32:7). He is going to bring you out with the victory (1 Corinthians 15:57; 2 Corinthians 2:14)!

I have prayed in advance for everyone who reads this book. As we embark on this journey together, this is what I believe and declare over you, according to God's promises:

- God is going to heal you completely, body and soul, and restore your health (Isaiah 53:4–5 csb; Psalm 103:2–3; Matthew 8:17; 1 Peter 2:24; 3 John 2).

- In all things, you are more than a conqueror, and you will conquer this medical condition (Romans 8:37).

- No weapon formed against you will prosper (Isaiah 54:17). This medical condition may have formed against you, but in the end it will not prevail.
- You are not in this fight alone. The God of the universe is with you and for you. He's fighting your battles and leaning into you with His grace (2 Chronicles 20:15; 2 Corinthians 12:9).
- According to Proverbs 4:18, your path is shining brighter and brighter until the full day. Your brightest days and greatest victories are still in your future.
- Your latter days will be greater than your former days. The rest of your life will be the best of your life (Job 42:12).
- With long life God will satisfy you and show you His salvation (Psalm 91:16).

Get your faith and expectancy up! God is about to turn your situation around and do something amazing in your life!

Before we get started, I want to address something even more important than your healing—your eternal salvation. A physical healing may last a lifetime, but your eternal destiny is forever. If you have never asked Jesus to be your Lord and Savior, or if you want to rededicate your life to Him, there is no better time than right now. Don't miss out on anything God has for you, especially your salvation. I invite you to pray this simple prayer from your heart:

### Prayer of Salvation or Rededication

Jesus, I believe You died on the cross for my sins and eternal salvation is found in You alone. I ask You to come into my heart and be my Lord and Savior. I give You my life and desire to follow You the rest of my days. Thank You for the free gift of salvation and that my eternal destiny is secure. In Your precious name I pray, Amen.

If you prayed that prayer, the Bible says you were born again spiritually. Not only are you guaranteed eternal life with God in heaven, but all of God's promises belong to you, including healing. Let's go . . . your healing awaits!

# DAY 1

## Anchored in Hope

This hope we have as an anchor of the soul, both sure and steadfast.

Hebrews 6:19

Hope is a very powerful and indispensable force. The Bible says, "Faith is the substance of things hoped for" (Hebrews 11:1). We can't have faith unless we first have hope. Hope is the oxygen of faith. Proverbs 13:12 says, "Hope deferred makes the heart sick." In my experience, when people who are battling an illness lose hope, they usually decline rapidly and eventually die. So it is vital to keep hope alive in your heart. The way to do that is to not anchor your hope in the doctors, medicine, test results, or anything in the natural. God uses doctors and medicine, but He alone is your Healer and Deliverer, and He is not limited to anything in the natural. He's a supernatural God. Keep your eyes on Him and your hope anchored in Him alone.

There is a natural hope—hoping the doctors can help you, the test results are good, the treatment works, the surgery is successful, your body responds well. There is nothing wrong with this kind of hope, but it depends on the uncertainties of natural circumstances. When our hope is anchored in the natural, we can succumb to fear, doubt, discouragement, and disappointment. But there is a hope in God that supersedes natural hope. When our hope is anchored in God, we can have an inner peace and rest knowing that even if we have setbacks and things don't go our way, God is on the throne and in control. He has us in the palm of His hand, and everything will be okay in the end.

One of the things I have loved about ministering to the sick for the last 25 years is having a front-row seat to countless miracles God has done in people's lives. I wish I had a dollar for every time the doctors said there was nothing more they could do and God worked a miraculous healing. Often, God does His greatest miracles when there is no more hope in the natural because then only He gets the credit. I think about my friend Austin, a 42-year-old tech CEO. In late 2021, he went to the doctor for a routine physical, which his wife made him undergo every year. He had no symptoms in his body and felt fine. To his utter shock, the doctor said he saw signs of possible liver cancer and referred him to an oncologist.

After seeing an oncologist and further testing, it was concluded that he had stage 4 liver cancer that had already spread to his brain, kidneys, and lymph nodes. Four top doctors, including his oncologist at MD Anderson Cancer Center, gave him a virtual death sentence. For nine months, he kept getting negative reports from doctors. But Austin and his wife's hope was anchored in God.

They refused to passively accept the negative reports and chose to believe God's Word instead, which says that Austin was healed by the stripes of Jesus and that no weapon formed against him would prosper. They dug their heels in and declared God's healing promises over Austin multiple times a day, praying bold, faith-filled prayers. Every time fear, doubt, or discouragement tried to come in, they actively resisted those thoughts and emotions, replacing them with truth from God's Word.

Three weeks before he returned to MD Anderson in Houston for more testing, he got a PET scan, which showed the cancer was no longer responding to chemo and had gotten worse. We met before his testing at MD Anderson, and I prayed over him. After two days of PET scans, blood work, and other testing, Austin sent me the following text:

> Steve, we have been witnesses to the most amazing miracle of my life: my scan was completely clean. NO CANCER ANYWHERE IN MY BODY!! We are completely stunned and speechless. We are just in awe of what God is doing. The

doctor says he has never seen anything like this. The surgeon said the same thing. He recommends I do not have surgery since he does not think it is necessary. Praise and thanks be to God!!!!!!!! Thank you so much for your support!!

Given the scan three weeks earlier that showed his cancer had worsened, only God could have done this miracle. Even the doctors said there was no medical explanation. As of the writing of this devotional, Austin has gotten monthly scans for eleven months and is still cancer free.

Keep your hope anchored in God alone. He can do things that doctors and medicine can't. Don't allow yourself to deify doctors and act as if their word is gospel. Don't hang your hopes on mortal men and medicine. God alone is your Healer, He has the final say, and His report trumps all others.

---

Father, Your Word tells us not to put our trust in mortal man but in You alone [see Psalm 146:3; Jeremiah 17:5; Psalm 118:9; Isaiah 2:22]. Thank You that You are my Healer and Deliverer, that You have all power and nothing is impossible with You. You use doctors and medicine, but You are not limited to these resources. You can do things doctors and medicine can't do. I put my hope in You alone and believe You for my complete healing, wholeness, and restoration. In Jesus' mighty name, Amen.

# DAY 2

# God of the Impossible

[God] performs wonders that cannot be fathomed, miracles
that cannot be counted.

Job 5:9 NIV

O ne of my favorite things about ministering to the
sick for many years is having a front-row seat to
see God do countless amazing miracles. I've seen
God heal blind, deaf, and paralyzed people instantly. I have
lost count of how many tumors have vanished. I've seen every
kind of disease miraculously healed, often when doctors
said there was nothing more they could do. I've even seen
people rally back after being taken off life support. I'm here
to testify that there is absolutely nothing too hard for our
God! The word *impossible* is not in His vocabulary. What

we call "impossible," God does naturally and effortlessly. Stretch your faith and believe God for your miracle!

When God led the Israelites out of slavery in Egypt, they had no doctors, hospitals, MRI machines, or pharmacies. And yet for forty years in the wilderness, God made sure that not one person out of more than two million Israelites was sick or weak (Psalm 105:37). He's a supernatural God. He can do what doctors and medicine can't do. If you are a Bible-believing Christian, you know that God created the whole universe with the words of His mouth, parted the Red Sea, raised Jesus from the dead, and did countless other astonishing miracles. The same God who did all these things can take care of whatever sickness or condition you have!

My friend Ramiro was born without ears. Doctors told his parents he would probably never hear or speak. They took him to specialists, and they all said the same thing. One day, his mother was holding Ramiro in her arms and crying. His grandmother, who is a faith-filled prayer warrior, walked into the room and said, "God is going to turn this around and heal Ramiro." Nothing changed for a while, and Ramiro started learning sign language as a toddler. Undaunted, his grandmother and parents kept praying bold prayers and declaring that God was going to heal him. After a while, Ramiro started responding to noises. Doctors were also able to reconstruct the outer part of his ears. At fifteen, Ramiro started singing. God healed him so completely that today he is one of the worship leaders at Lakewood Church, the largest church in America. He explained that to be a worship leader, you have to hear perfectly, sing in the right key, and pronounce words clearly—all of which are a miracle for someone doctors said would never hear or speak. But God wasn't done. Ramiro auditioned for *American Idol*. Not only did the show share his healing testimony, but he sang "Amazing Grace" and got a golden ticket to Hollywood! Ramiro said, "People will try to box you in and tell you what you can't do, but God has the final say. If He did it for me, He can do it for you!"

Sometimes God will bring us to a place where the odds are stacked against us and it looks impossible in the natural because He wants to do a greater miracle. When God freed the Israelites from Egypt, He led them to the Red Sea. I have looked at a map of their route, and it would have been much quicker and easier if He had led them the short distance north around the Red Sea, but He didn't. He led them to a place where they were trapped—with the Red Sea on one side and the Egyptian army bearing down on the other. It was a setup for God to do one of His greatest miracles—parting the Red Sea. When Jesus' friend Lazarus was deathly ill, they sent word to Jesus, who was in another town, to come quickly.

> [Jesus] said, "This sickness is not unto death, but for the glory of God." . . . So, when He heard that he was sick, He stayed two more days in the place where He was. . . . Then

Jesus said to them plainly, "Lazarus is dead. And I am glad for your sakes that I was not there, that you may believe. Nevertheless let us go to him."

John 11:4, 6, 14–15

Jesus deliberately delayed going to Lazarus for two days. They were hoping for a healing, but Jesus wanted to do something far greater—a resurrection! When God is taking longer to heal you than you hoped, trust Him. He knows what He's doing. Keep standing. Keep believing. Keep declaring. God has a miracle with your name on it, and your faith will cause it to manifest in His perfect timing!

Heavenly Father, thank You that You are a God of miracles and that nothing is impossible with You! Thank You that my miracle is on the way! In Jesus's name, Amen.

# DAY 3

## All Inclusive

He himself bore our sicknesses . . . and we are healed by
his wounds.

Isaiah 53:4–5 csb

I heard a story about a man who took a transatlantic trip on a cruise liner in the early days. Every day, he ate cheese and crackers on the deck while others ate at the extravagant buffet inside. One day, someone said, "I notice you're always out here eating cheese and crackers. Why don't you come in and eat with us?" "My ticket doesn't include meals," the man replied. "Every ticket includes meals," the person said. The man was ecstatic and dined like a king for the rest of the trip.

Many Christians are like this man. They have salvation but aren't enjoying its full benefits. All they've been taught about Jesus' death is that He died for our sins so we could have eternal salvation. If that was all He did, it would have been enough and worthy of our eternal praise. But there is so much more included in our salvation than just a ticket to heaven. *Your Jesus ticket is all inclusive!* Jesus didn't just come to earth to save us in the "sweet by and by" but leave us sick, broke, and defeated here. He came to heal us, set us free, and give us abundant life (John 10:10)!

When God created Adam and Eve, there was no sin and no separation from God. They had perfect fellowship with Him. There was also no sickness, death, or lack in the Garden. This was God's vision for humankind. But everything changed when Adam and Eve sinned. Man was now eternally separated from God because He is perfect and holy and cannot be in the presence of sin. Our sin and separation from God ushered into the world sickness, death, lack, and many other plights. Jesus came to the earth to reconcile us to God and restore His original vision for humankind. In the Lord's Prayer, He taught us to pray, "Your kingdom come. Your will be done on earth as it is in heaven." God's Kingdom does not have sickness, and sickness was never His will for us. There is no sickness in heaven, and there was no sickness in the Garden. So when Jesus died on the cross, He not only paid the price for our sins but for everything that came into the world because of sin, including sickness. Let's look at what the Bible says.

In a prophecy about Jesus eight hundred years before His death, Isaiah 53:4 says, "He himself bore our sicknesses, and he carried our pains . . . and we are healed by his wounds" (CSB). Matthew 8:17 restates this passage and makes it even clearer: "This was to fulfill what was spoken through the prophet Isaiah: 'He took up our infirmities and bore our diseases'" (NIV). Psalm 103:2–3 also affirms that healing was part of Jesus's salvation work on the cross: "Bless the LORD, O my soul, and forget not all His benefits: *who forgives all your iniquities, who heals all your diseases*." And finally, 1 Peter 2:24 pairs salvation and physical healing: "[Jesus] bore our sins in His own body on the tree . . . by whose stripes you were healed." Notice this verse is in the past tense: we *were* healed by Jesus' stripes two thousand years ago. He already bore our sicknesses and paid the price with His life for our healing.

Hebrews 6:9 says, "Beloved, we are confident of better things concerning you, yes, *things that accompany salvation*." It is clear from the above passages that healing is one of the things that accompany salvation. The Greek word for "salvation" is the noun *soteria*. The verb form "to save" is *sozo*. It means to save and rescue *spiritually and physically*, to *heal and deliver*; restoration to a state of safety, soundness, *health*, and *well-being*, as well as preservation from danger of destruction.[1] Stir up your faith to receive the healing that Jesus already paid for and watch it manifest in your body.

———  ——  ———

Heavenly Father, thank You that Jesus not only bore my sins in His own body at the cross, but He bore my sicknesses, diseases, and pains upon Himself. By His stripes I was healed two thousand years ago. My healing was already paid for by the precious blood of Jesus. By faith, I receive my complete healing, wholeness, and restoration. In Jesus's mighty name, Amen.

# DAY 4

## Just Receive

Ask, and you will receive, that your joy may be made full.

John 16:24

People are always talking about wanting to get their healing or breakthrough. The truth is, it's not about trying to get God to move but just receiving by faith what He's already promised. We're not trying to get something from God. We're not trying to persuade God to move. We don't need to beg, plead, cajole, or twist God's arm. We don't have to perform or be good enough for God's blessings. God has already given us everything. Jesus has already paid the price on the cross for our healing. Our job is to get into agreement with what He's done and His promises and receive them by faith. Second Corinthians 1:20 says, "For no matter how many promises God has made, they are 'Yes' in Christ. And so through him the 'Amen' is spoken by us to the glory of God" (NIV). God has already said "Yes" to your healing. All you have to do is give Him your "Amen" ("so be it") agreement and receive it by faith.

It's like our salvation. Jesus already did it all on the cross. He did all the heavy lifting. In His own words, "It is finished" (John 19:30). There is nothing we can do to add to Jesus' finished work on the cross. All we have to do is *believe* and *receive*. It is only by faith, not works, that we receive the free gift of salvation. The same is true about our healing. Jesus already bore our sicknesses upon Himself at the cross, and by His stripes we *were* healed two thousand years ago (Isaiah 53:4–5; Matthew 8:17; 1 Peter 2:24). He already paid the price for our healing. All we have to do is receive it by faith. This doesn't mean it will manifest the moment we have faith. I have seen many instant healings, but most of the time God takes us through a process. I believe that's because He's trying to do a work in us beyond just our physical healing. He's trying to develop our faith and other spiritual muscles, our character, and a deeper relationship with Him. We don't get these things without walking through some adversity. They are developed in the valley, not on the mountaintop.

My favorite healing story in the Bible is about the woman with the issue of blood in Mark 5:25–34. This woman had a bleeding condition for twelve years and had spent all her money on doctors, but she only got worse (Mark 5:26). She heard Jesus was coming to her town and kept saying to herself, "If only I may touch His clothes, I shall be made well" (Mark 5:28).[1] What is interesting is when she encountered Jesus, she didn't cry out to Him. She didn't beg Jesus and say, "Please heal me, Jesus!" In fact, they did not exchange words at all. She simply touched the hem of Jesus' garment, and the Bible says her faith drew the healing power out of Him (Mark 5:30, 34). The healing power was already there; all she had to do was receive it by faith.

Children know how to receive. I have two daughters, and every time I have given them something, not once have they ever said, "Dad, I'm not worthy. I'm a sinner. I don't deserve it." Children aren't hindered by reasonings or feelings of guilt and unworthiness. They just receive. But adults often reason away receiving the blessings of God. We entertain lies that we're not good enough, we've made too many mistakes, or we need to perform for God's approval and blessings. Jesus said we need to become like a child (Matthew 18:3). Today, cease striving and know that He is God (Psalm 46:10 NASB). Just receive by faith your healing, which Jesus already paid for with His life, and keep believing until it manifests.

Father God, help me to receive by faith everything Jesus died to give me. I believe Your promise that Jesus bore all my sicknesses and infirmities on the cross and by His stripes I was healed. By faith, I receive divine healing,

25

wholeness, and restoration in every part of my body. Deliver me from any feelings of guilt, shame, condemnation and unworthiness, or performance-mindset, and help me to have a receiving mindset as a blood-bought, blood-washed child of God. In Jesus' precious name, Amen.

# DAY 5

# Healing Is a Choice

I have set before you life and death. . . . Choose life.

Deuteronomy 30:19

One time, Jesus was in Jerusalem for a Jewish feast when He encountered a man at the pool of Bethesda who had been unable to walk for 38 years (John 5:1–15). The pool was known for its healing powers because periodically an angel would stir the waters and whoever got in first would be healed. Someone always beat this man into the pool when it stirred, so he continued to lie there, waiting for his next opportunity. Jesus asked him a puzzling question: "Do you want to be made well?" (John 5:6). Clearly, the man was at a place people went for healing and the passage indicates Jesus knew how long he'd had that condition, so why would Jesus ask such an obvious question?

Implicit in Jesus' question is the fact that God needs our consent and cooperation. He doesn't force anything on us, not even salvation. Healing, like salvation, is a choice. You have an important part to play in receiving healing from God. My goal in this devotional and in my first book, *God Heals*, is to help you make choices that will position you to receive your healing.

I will never forget a man I ministered to weekly for about a year at MD Anderson Cancer Center. He was in his forties and had been diagnosed with stage 4 colon cancer. Every time I walked into his room, I noticed he had two or three Dr Peppers next to his bed. I also noticed his diet consisted of a lot of sugars and carbs, which cancer cells love. He and I became close friends, and eventually I felt the liberty to lovingly encourage him to lay off the sodas and modify his diet to help his body heal. The Scripture says, "Faith without works is dead" (James 2:20, 26). We have to put some works to our faith and give God something to work with. He expects us to take care of our temple and be good stewards of what He's given us. Unfortunately, my advice fell on deaf ears, and my friend passed away. I can't say for sure if the sodas and poor diet hindered his healing, but it always baffled me that he wasn't willing to do whatever it took to be healed. When you are battling for your health, perhaps even your life, every choice matters. You have to do your part and then trust God to do His part.

I ministered to another man at MD Anderson Cancer Center who was from a denomination that believes that divine healing is not for today, that it was only for the era of Jesus and His disciples. Nothing in the Bible supports this belief, but that's what he believed. The Bible and countless miracle healing testimonies from around the globe prove that God is a supernatural healing God and still heals today. This man acted like he was offended by my faith and thought I was some kind of snake oil salesman when I encouraged him to believe God for his healing. I don't know what ever happened with him, but I do know that Scripture says we can't receive anything from God without faith (James 1:6–7). If you want to receive divine healing from God, you may have to expand your theology some to align with the Bible and stretch your faith. God is so much bigger than our religion. Jesus said in Mark 9:23, "If you can believe, *all* things are possible to him who believes." If you can believe God for your healing, nothing is impossible with Him!

I have also ministered to a large swath of people who deify doctors and act like what they say is gospel, leaving little room for God in the equation. It is a symptom of the modern era and the fact that most churches don't teach about faith and healing that many people put more faith in doctors, medicine, information, and technology than in God. But God is a supernatural God, and He's not limited by anything in the natural. Doctors and medicine are limited, but He is not. I love what Dr. Paul Osteen, a surgeon and the brother of Pastor Joel Osteen, said: "Doctors treat but only God heals." Put your faith in God over anything else.

My encouragement to you as we take this forty-day journey together to reclaim your health is this: be open and willing to do whatever it takes to receive your healing. This is what has separated people I have seen receive a miracle healing from those who did not. Healing is a choice.

Father, help me to cooperate with You and make choices every day that will position me to receive my healing. In Jesus' mighty name, Amen.

# DAY 6

# Fighting from Victory

But thanks be to God, who gives us the victory through our
Lord Jesus Christ.

*1 Corinthians 15:57*

You may be in a serious battle for your health or have a loved one who is. When we go through a tough health challenge, especially a prolonged one, it can feel like the sickness or the enemy has the upper hand. Maybe you feel battle weary and like your faith is hanging on by a thread. But I want to remind you today that you already have the victory in Christ Jesus. You are not fighting *for* victory; you are fighting *from* victory. Jesus has already paid the price for your healing. You are not a sick person trying to get well, but a person who was healed by the stripes of

Jesus two thousand years ago and is now resisting sickness. It's so important to remind yourself of this every day and keep a victorious mindset. Let me wash you in the Word with God's promises of victory:

- "But thanks be to God, who gives us the victory through our Lord Jesus Christ" (1 Corinthians 15:57). God has already given us the victory. We still have battles to fight, but we are fighting from a position of victory. The battle is rigged in our favor!

- "Now thanks be to God who *always* leads us in triumph in Christ" (2 Corinthians 2:14). God always leads us in triumph, not just sometimes. He has never lost a battle, and He never will!

- "We are more than conquerors through Him who loved us" (Romans 8:37). A conqueror is someone who fights a battle and wins, but Paul says we are *more than conquerors*. That's because Jesus has already won the battle for us. We may still have to fight, but victory is certain.

- "Many are the afflictions of the righteous, but the LORD delivers him out of them *all*" (Psalm 34:19). God never said we wouldn't have afflictions. In fact, He said we would have many. But He promised to deliver us out of them *all*. And God always keeps His promises.

- "No weapon formed against you shall prosper" (Isaiah 54:17). A weapon may be formed against you—like this sickness—but it will not prosper. It may hurt and weaken you in the short term, but it will not prevail over you.

You may look anything *but* victorious right now, but don't go by how things look in the natural. "We walk by faith, and not by sight" (2 Corinthians 5:7). Faith has nothing to do with how things look to our natural eyes and mind. I have seen many people who looked hopeless in the natural, tubes coming out everywhere, even people on life support, and God miraculously turned their situations around. The doctor may not say you are victorious, but you must believe God's report over the doctor's. His report says you are healed by the stripes of Jesus, that no weapon formed against you shall prosper, and that He always leads you to triumph in Christ Jesus. You are fighting *from* victory, not *for* victory. You are a victor and never a victim. Don't allow yourself to entertain a victim mindset.

This is what David knew when he fought Goliath, a giant twice his size who was a professional fighter and armed to the teeth. David had no armor, and the only weapon he had was a slingshot. Not only that, Goliath had a shield bearer who went before him to shield him. Ridiculously lopsided and impossible odds in the natural. It would have been understandable if David had retreated in terror. But David knew he was fighting from a position of victory because God Almighty was on his side. He told Goliath, "You come to me with a sword, with a spear, and with a javelin. But I come to you in the name of the LORD of hosts. . . . This day the LORD will deliver you into my hand, and I will strike you and take your head from you" (1 Samuel 17:45–46). Then he ran at Goliath and struck him down with one smooth stone from his slingshot.

Like David, you are empowered by God to defeat every giant you face. He's given you everything you need to win the battle—the Word of God, faith, prayer, the blood of Jesus, the armor of God, and much more! The battle is rigged in your favor!

Father, thank You that You always lead me to triumph in Christ Jesus and deliver me out of all my troubles. It is only a matter of time before I emerge from this health challenge victorious. Help me to stay in faith and keep a victorious mindset. In Jesus' mighty name, Amen.

# DAY 7

# Boundless Love

Look with wonder at the depth of the Father's marvelous love that he has lavished on us! He has called us and made us his very own beloved children.

1 John 3:1 TPT

Walking through a serious health challenge, especially a prolonged one, presents ample opportunities to have thoughts like, *Why me? Where is God? Why hasn't God healed me yet? Maybe God doesn't care. Maybe God is mad at me. Maybe I don't deserve to be healed.* Many patients have shared these kinds of thoughts and emotions with me. Even Jesus in His humanity said, "My God, My God, why have You forsaken Me?" (Matthew 27:46) as He hung on the cross. David expressed similar sentiments in the psalms: "Why do You stand afar off, O LORD? Why do You hide in times of trouble?" (Psalm 10:1). "How long, O LORD? Will You forget me forever?" (Psalm 13:1). All the greats in the Bible had moments like this. So if you have felt like this at times, it doesn't mean you are weak or a bad Christian; it means you are human. I want to remind you today how much God loves and adores you. God is not mad at you; He's madly in love with you. You are His beloved child. His pearl of great price. The one He sacrificed His only Son for. God knows everything about you—the good, the bad, the ugly—and He still loves and accepts you unconditionally. Nothing can separate you from His love. He will never leave you, nor forsake you. He has great plans for your life!

This is critical to remember in your healing journey, because how can you have faith to receive your healing from someone you think is mad at you or doesn't love or care about you very much? I pray that you open your heart wide and receive God's love. Meditate on it. Declare it. Soak in it. Let it permeate every fiber of your being. Let it resound in your spirit and soul in the tough times. Let it be louder than the enemy's lies. Louder than your weary thoughts and emotions. Louder than your fears. Even when you don't consciously feel His love, it is there. He is covering you with His love and carrying you in His arms. The Scripture says, "Praise the Lord; praise God our savior! For each day he carries us in his arms" (Psalm 68:19 NLT).

Sometimes people have a skewed perception of God because of how they were raised, traumas they have experienced, or other reasons. I pray that you see God how He really is. He is not cold, aloof, and uncaring. He is not a harsh religious overlord. He is your loving heavenly Father. The Scripture says, "See what great love the Father has lavished on us, that we should be called children of God!" (1 John 3:1 NIV). You don't have to earn His love. It is a free gift. Before Jesus started His ministry or did a single miracle, God's voice boomed from heaven and said, "This is My beloved Son in whom I am well-pleased." He loved Jesus and was proud of Him simply because Jesus was His Son, not because of anything He did. God is saying the same thing to you today: "You are My beloved child in whom I am well-pleased."

God's love is not just demonstrated by the end result of your healing, but in countless ways throughout the journey. My friend Connie was diagnosed with the most aggressive form of ovarian cancer, and it had metastasized to her colon. It took a year for her to get diagnosed and begin treatment. It was a miracle she lived through that first year. She went through months of chemo treatments, and God totally healed her. She has been cancer free for eleven years. She said, "During my ordeal, I experienced God's love like never before. It's one thing to know God loves you when everything is good; it's another thing to see His love in action when you're walking through the darkest valley. He showed His love for me every day—comforting me when I was afraid, strengthening me when I was weak, reminding me of His promises when my faith was wobbly, bringing the right doctors and health-care workers into my life, and countless other ways. He not only healed my body; He healed my soul. I would tell anybody going through a health challenge that God's love for you has no limits and will never fail. His love will carry you through to victory."

Heavenly Father, thank You for Your amazing, unconditional love that You have lavished on me that I should be called Your child. Help me to receive the fullness of Your love. In Jesus' name, Amen.

# Reflections and Prayers

What are your key takeaways from the past seven days?

_____

_____

_____

_____

_____

Based on those takeaways, what action steps could you implement to help your journey to healing?

_____

_____

_____

_____

_____

Use this space to write your current prayer requests to God and anything God has spoken to you about your situation through His Word, the Holy Spirit, people, dreams, or other means.

# DAY 8

# Your Most Important Identity

As he thinks in his heart, so is he.

Proverbs 23:7

Few things can challenge a person's identity like battling a serious illness. Recently, a hospital patient shared with me how she was not able to function normally in her role as a wife, mother, daughter, sibling, and friend. She couldn't serve her family the way she used to, go to work and do her job, or volunteer at her church. These roles were key parts of her identity, and now they were in limbo. She felt a loss of identity. In her mind, she was just a sick person now. I'm going to tell you what I told her. Your most important identity—and one that never changes—is that you are a child of the Most High God. Circumstances may change, but your identity and value in Christ never changes.

As you journey toward your healing, there will be other dynamics at work trying to challenge your identity in Christ. Medical personnel and perhaps those in your circle see you as a sick person. And, of course, the enemy is always trying to push the wrong identity on us. He wants you to identify as a sick, fearful victim. Your own thoughts and emotions may try to push you into the wrong identity. That's why it is so important to remind yourself every day of who you are in Christ. After today's devotional, there is a list of "I am" statements based on Scripture to remind you of your identity in Christ. Read and meditate on them often. Let them penetrate deep into your spirit. Saturate yourself in who you are in Christ. When your identity is rooted firmly in Christ, nothing can shake you.

So many people allow their sickness or condition to become a part of their identity. It dominates their thoughts, conversations, and prayers. Their whole life starts to revolve around it. And I understand it. I'm not being judgmental or critical. I'm just saying you can't allow your condition to swallow up your identity. You have to reject it. Don't receive it as yours. It doesn't belong to you. It is trespassing. Don't let it become part of your identity. You have to enforce your identity and rights in Christ. You are a child of the Most High God, healed by the stripes of Jesus. Divine health is part of your inheritance, paid for by the precious blood of Jesus. You are not a sick person trying to get well, but a healthy person resisting sickness. Don't say things like, "I have cancer," "my cancer," or "I'm a diabetic." Instead, say, "I am overcoming cancer/diabetes/whatever." Or "I was diagnosed with such and such, but God is healing me." Your words have power. Rather than claiming the sickness every time you tell someone about it, use every opportunity to claim your healing. Reinforce your identity and inheritance in Christ as often as you can.

You may be in a situation that contradicts what God's Word promises you. He promised that you were healed by the stripes of Jesus, but you are battling a serious illness. He promised you abundant life, but maybe your life feels anything but abundant. Your job is to hold on to what God promised you and what He says about you. This is what Joseph had to do. God gave him two dreams about being in a high position, but right after those dreams, his jealous brothers sold him into slavery in Egypt. For thirteen years, Joseph was a slave in Potiphar's house and then a prisoner after being falsely accused by Potiphar's wife. He could easily have given in to bitterness and self-pity, but Joseph did not allow the pit to change his identity or what he believed. He stayed positive, kept trusting God, and held on to his identity. Finally, God came through, and in one day Joseph went from the prison to the palace when Pharoah made him the prime minister of Egypt. That's how quickly God can change things. *How you see yourself in the pit will determine how well you come out of the pit.* The pit doesn't change what God promised you or your God-given identity. You are a child of God in the pit. You are royalty in the pit. You have God's DNA and royal blood flowing through your veins. God has crowned you with His favor. Nothing can ever change that. Circumstances, people, and your environment don't determine your identity; God does. See yourself as God sees you. If you hold on to your identity in Christ and His promises, your miracle breakthrough is on the way!

Father, thank You for my identity in Christ and that nothing can ever change it. In Jesus' name, Amen.

# My Identity in Christ

**I am** a child of the Most High God. (1 John 3:1; John 1:12; Romans 8:16)

**I am** made in the image and likeness of God. (Genesis 1:27)

**I am** fearfully and wonderfully made. (Psalm 139:14)

**I am** a unique masterpiece handcrafted by the Creator of the universe. (Ephesians 2:10)

**I am** the apple of God's eye. (Psalm 17:8)

**I am** passionately and unconditionally loved by God. (1 John 3:1; Romans 5:8; 1 John 4:9–10)

**I am** eternally saved by grace, not by my own merit, works, or performance. (Ephesians 2:8)

**I am** forgiven and cleansed of all my sins. (Colossians 1:14; 1 Corinthians 6:11)

**I am** the righteousness of God in Christ Jesus. (2 Corinthians 5:21)

**I am** holy and blameless before God because of the blood of Jesus. (Ephesians 1:4)

**I am** accepted by God. (Ephesians 1:6)

**I am** a new creation in Christ. (2 Corinthians 5:17)

**I am** complete in Christ. (Colossians 2:10)

**I am** one spirit with Christ. (1 Corinthians 6:17)

**I am** the temple of the Holy Spirit. (1 Corinthians 3:16)

**I am** a citizen of heaven. (Philippians 3:20)

**I am** an heir of the kingdom of God. (Romans 8:17)

**I am** an heir according to the blessing of Abraham. (Galatians 3:13–14)

**I am** blessed with every spiritual blessing. (Ephesians 1:3)

**I am** healed by the stripes of Jesus—spirit, soul, and body. (1 Peter 2:24)

**I am** a healthy person resisting sickness, not a sick person trying to get well. (Isaiah 53:4–5 NIV; Matthew 8:17; 1 Peter 2:24)

**I am** more than a conqueror in all things. (Romans 8:37)

**I am** a victor and not a victim. I am always victorious in Christ. (1 Corinthians 15:57; 2 Corinthians 2:14)

**I am** delivered from the powers of darkness. (Colossians 1:13)

**I am** seated with Christ in heavenly places far above all powers of darkness. (Ephesians 2:6)

**I am** free from every yoke of bondage. (Galatians 5:1)

**I am** free from fear. (Romans 8:15; 2 Timothy 1:7)

**I am** strong in the Lord and the power of His might. (Ephesians 6:10)

**I am** filled with the Holy Spirit. (Ephesians 5:18)

**I am** led by the Holy Spirit in all things. (Romans 8:14)

**I am** being renewed in the spirit (attitude) of my mind. (Ephesians 4:23)

**I am** a doer of the Word, not just a hearer. (James 1:22)

**I am** protected by God's angels. (Psalm 34:7; Psalm 91:11–12)

**I am** sufficient and able to do whatever God calls me to do. (2 Corinthians 3:5; 1 Peter 4:11)

# DAY 9

# Magnify God over Your Sickness

My soul magnifies the Lord.

Luke 1:46

The word *magnify* means "to make bigger." When we magnify an object by holding a magnifying glass up to it, it appears much larger than it is. What we focus on becomes magnified in our minds. When we focus on our problems, they become huge, scary, and overwhelming. But the more we focus on God and magnify Him in our minds, the smaller our problems become. The truth is, God is bigger, higher, and stronger than any problem we face. I'm asking you to keep your focus on God and magnify Him over your medical condition. One of the most powerful choices we have in life is what we focus on. That one choice alone could be decisive to your outcome.

One person can get a bad medical report and obsess on their condition and what the doctor said. They'll think, *The doctor said such and such. I don't know if I can overcome this* or *I don't know if God will heal me.* Another person will get the exact same diagnosis and think, *My God is bigger than this sickness. He has all power. He is well able to heal me. He said I am healed by the stripes of Jesus and no weapon formed against me shall prosper.* Which of these two people do you think is most likely to be healed? You get to choose which one you will be. It's all about what you magnify in your mind—the sickness and the doctor's report or God and His report.

When Moses sent the twelve spies to spy out the Promised Land, they all saw the exact same thing. It was the very best land—an incredibly fertile oasis flowing with milk and honey and big, luscious produce. The God of the universe had promised to give them this land and help them defeat the current occupants. But instead of focusing on God and His promise and all the good in the land, ten of the spies fixated on the large size of the people who lived there. They said, "We are not able to go up against the people, for they are stronger than we. . . . We saw the giants . . . and we were like grasshoppers in our own sight, and so we were in their sight" (Numbers 13:31–33). The King James Version calls this an "evil report" (v. 32). Two of the spies, Joshua and Caleb, saw the exact same thing, but said, "Let us go up at once and take possession, for we are well able to overcome it" (v. 30). And guess what? Those two spies were the only ones out of that entire generation of over two million Israelites who made it into the Promised Land because they focused on God instead of the problem.

When David faced the nine-foot giant Goliath, he didn't focus on the size of Goliath. Everybody else called Goliath a "giant," but not David. He called him an "uncircumcised Philistine." Everybody else said, "He's too big to defeat." David said, "He's too big to miss." How could David have so much confidence when everybody else was terrified? Because everybody else was focused on the size of the problem, and David was focused on the size of his God. He told Goliath, "You come against me with sword and spear and javelin, but I come against you in the name of the LORD Almighty. . . . This day the LORD will deliver you into my hands" (1 Samuel 17:45–46 NIV).

When God promised Abraham and Sarah a baby, they were elderly and way past childbearing years. But the Scripture says:

> Not being weak in faith, [Abraham] *did not consider* his own body, already dead (since he was about a hundred years old), and the deadness of Sarah's womb. *He did not waver* at the promise of God through unbelief, but was strengthened in faith, giving glory to God, and being *fully convinced* that what He had promised He was also able to perform.
>
> Romans 4:19–21

Abraham was focused on the bigness and power of God rather than the natural impossibility of him and Sarah having a child at their age. Instead of considering your circumstances and what the doctor said, why don't you consider your God? He spoke worlds into existence. He flung the stars into space. He parted the Red Sea. He healed people of every kind of sickness and raised the dead throughout the Bible, and He never changes. He's a Way Maker, Miracle Worker, Promise Keeper. He can make a way where there seems to be no way.

Father God, help me to keep my focus on You and magnify You over my medical condition. In Jesus' mighty name, Amen.

# DAY 10

## Whose Report
## Will You Believe?

Who has believed the report of the Lord?

Isaiah 53:1, author's paraphrase

When battling an illness, you are presented with all kinds of reports. There is the doctor's report—his or her findings and prognosis. There is the enemy's report. He doesn't want you healed, so he will whisper lies in your mind: *You're never going to get better. God doesn't care about you. If He did, He would have healed you by now. You might as well give up. You don't deserve to be healed after the life you've lived.* There is the report of your family and friends. Everybody has an opinion and faith perspective depending on their walk with God (or lack thereof). People don't mean to bring harm to your life, but their report can often be carnal and riddled with doubt. Then there is the report of your own mind, which includes all the fears, imaginations, doubts, and "what-if's" coursing through your mind. Finally—and most importantly—there is God's report. His report says that Jesus already bore your sicknesses upon Himself at the cross and by His stripes you were healed, that God heals *all* your diseases, that no weapon formed against you shall prosper, that in all things you are more than a conqueror, and that God will deliver you and satisfy you with a long life (Isaiah 53:4–5 CSB; Matthew 8:17; 1 Peter 2:24; Psalm 103:3; Isaiah 54:17; Romans 8:37; Psalm 91:16). The choice is yours and yours alone: Whose report among all these competing reports will you believe?

By far, the most common stumbling block I have seen to people's faith and them receiving their healing is believing the wrong report, especially deifying doctors and making their report like gospel. So many people act like if the doctor said it, that's the way it's going to be. The doctor's report becomes their prevailing truth instead of what God said. I wish I had a dollar for every time doctors were wrong or God overrode them. In no way am I trying to diminish doctors. God uses doctors, health-care workers, and medicine powerfully, and many people wouldn't be alive today without them. But they are only humans, they don't get it right fairly often, and they don't have the final say. God does. He's not limited by doctors and medicine. He's a supernatural God.

He spoke the whole universe into existence.

He gave Abraham and Sarah a baby at one hundred and ninety years old.

He parted the Red Sea.

He rained manna from heaven for the Israelites.

He made the sun stand still for Joshua and his army.

He delivered the five Hebrew boys from the fiery furnace.

He protected Daniel in the lions' den.

He healed countless people of every kind of sickness and disease throughout the Bible.

He raised many people from the dead in the Bible.[1]

He caused Mary to give birth to Jesus without her first knowing a man.

He multiplied five loaves and two fish and fed over five thousand people.

If you had asked the experts if they thought any of these things were possible, they would have scoffed.

But God specialized in defying the odds.

He's the same yesterday, today, and forever. He never changes (Hebrews 13:8; James 1:17).

"He performs wonders that cannot be fathomed, miracles that cannot be counted" (Job 5:9 NIV).

He's not going to consult with your doctors or contemplate your test results before healing you. He is God Almighty, and He's not limited by anything in the natural.

The determining factor is not what people say. They don't control your destiny.

Pastor Joel Osteen told about his grandmother, who lived in the country and was feisty. She even chewed tobacco and had a spittoon. One day, she had a doctor's appointment, and the doctor said, "I'm sorry to tell you this, Mrs. Osteen, but you have Parkinson's disease." She immediately got up off the examining table and said, "Listen here, Doctor. I do not have Parkinson's, and besides, I'm too old to have Parkinson's." She lived out the rest of her days without having Parkinson's.

I'm not telling you to be unwise and deny the natural facts and pretend like nothing is wrong with you. I'm saying that God's truth supersedes the natural facts; His power prevails over doctors and medicine. But to appropriate His truth and power and receive your healing, you have to believe God's report above all others. Every day, you have to decide what you are going to believe and how you are going to think.

Father, help me to believe Your report above all others, in Jesus' mighty name, Amen.

# DAY 11

# This Is Only a Test

> The LORD tests the righteous.
>
> Psalm 11:5

We all go through times of adversity when the quality of our faith, character, and walk with God is tested by fire. The Scripture says, "Beloved, do not be surprised at the fiery trial when it comes upon you to test you, as though something strange were happening to you" (1 Peter 4:12 ESV). God doesn't bring sickness and adversity, but He allows them to test and develop us. Before Jesus began His public ministry, "The Holy Spirit led [him] into the desert, so that the devil could test[1] him" (Matthew 4:1 CEV). Notice it was the Holy Spirit who led

Jesus into the wilderness to be tested. God ordains times of testing for everyone, even Jesus.

It's easy to get discouraged or frustrated, think our situation is so unfair, and wonder why things aren't changing. But these times of testing show what is really inside of us and help us grow. *When God is not changing the circumstances, He is using the circumstances to change us.*

Peter swore that he would never deny Jesus when he was with Jesus and the other disciples and everything was fine. But the moment Jesus was arrested and things got hard, he publicly denied Jesus. We will never know what is really inside of us until we are put to the test. We will never know the true quality of our faith until we are in a good fight. Real faith is proven in the furnace of affliction. When everything is wonderful in our lives, we don't need faith. We will know what kind of faith we have not because we never went through anything, but because we went through a real trial and maintained our faith and grew in character while we persevered.

Job was described as a "blameless and upright" man who "feared God and shunned evil" (Job 1:1). He was doing everything right, but God still allowed his faith and character to be tested. It does not matter how long we have been a Christian, how godly we are, or how much we pray and study the Bible. It does not matter how wealthy, talented, attractive, or anointed we are. There comes a time in everyone's life when everything we believe and everything we say we are is put to the test. Jesus said, "Everyone will be tested with fire" (Mark 9:49 NLT).

Job lost everything—his family, health, and all his possessions—but his response is an example to us. He said, "Though [God] slay me, yet will I trust Him" (Job 13:15). His wife told him to just curse God and die, but he refused to do it. His so-called friends blamed him for his circumstances, but Job kept his peace and prayed for them. He said, "When [God] has tested me, I shall come forth as gold" (Job 23:10). And guess what? Because he kept his faith and passed the test, God not only restored his health, but He gave him back double everything he lost.

I ministered to a man who had cancer in his brain and several parts of his body for a year. He was like a modern-day Job. He endured brain surgeries and whole brain radiation, lung radiation, chemotherapy, immunotherapy, clinical drug trials, blood transfusions, plasma transfusions, hearing loss, vision loss, the shingles, ports, IVs, spinal taps, countless days spent in the hospital, hundreds of doctor visits, enough medications to fill a pharmacy, ambulance rides, physical therapy, occupational therapy, acupuncture, and many other things. But through it all, his joy and faith were unwavering. He always joked with the nurses and doctors and lifted everyone else up. Even when he felt horrible, he stayed positive and full of faith. I ministered to him every week, but the truth is he ministered way more to me.

Pass the test. Give God something to work with every day.

Wake up every morning and thank God for another day of life.

Put on the garment of praise for the spirit of heaviness.

Speak healing, life, and victory out of your mouth.

Stay positive and reject fear, doubt, and negativity.

Feed your spirit every day by reading the Word and listening to praise music.

Keep your faith stirred up with good preaching (online or in person).

This is when everything in your Christian life matters the most.

Pass the test, and you will see God move mightily in your life!

---

Father God, help me to pass the test and lead me on the path of healing and victory. In Jesus' name, Amen.

# DAY 12

# Fireproof

When you walk through the fire, you shall not be burned,
nor shall the flame scorch you.

Isaiah 43:2

One of my favorite stories in the Bible is about the
three Hebrew boys in Daniel 3 who were thrown
into a fiery furnace for worshiping God. The furnace was made so hot on the king's orders that it killed the
men who threw them into the fire. God not only protected
the three boys from the fire, but He was in the fire with them
as the preincarnate Jesus. When the king looked, he said,
"I see four men loose, walking in the midst of the fire; and
they are not hurt, and the form of the fourth is like the Son
of God" (Daniel 3:25).

Those boys emerged from the fire totally unscathed. Their clothes weren't burned. Their hair wasn't singed. They didn't even have the smell of smoke (Daniel 3:27). Nobody could tell they had ever been in a fire. They didn't look like what they had been through. You may be in a fire right now; but know for certain that God is with you in the fire and He will not allow it to consume you. He will make you fireproof. Isaiah 43:1–3 says, "Fear not, for I have redeemed you; I have called you by your name; you are Mine. . . . *When you walk through the fire, you shall not be burned, nor shall the flame scorch you.* For I am the LORD your God, the Holy One of Israel, your Savior."

When God restores your health, you're not going to look like what you went through. He's going to bring you out better than you were before, wiser and with greater faith and a deeper walk with Him. He will turn to your advantage what was meant for your harm. Romans 8:28 says, "*All* things work together for good to those who love God, to those who are the called according to His purpose."

My friend Melinda is a two-time cancer survivor. The second time, she was near death when I went to pray for her in the hospital. But God totally healed her, and the cancer has never returned. Another friend had severe cirrhosis of the liver from years of alcoholism and needed an urgent liver transplant. When I saw her in the hospital, she was teetering on the brink of death and bloated to twice her normal size with edema because her kidneys weren't working. God not only miraculously healed her enough to have the liver transplant surgery, but He provided her with a perfect liver at the last minute. He also radically delivered her from alcohol. Today, both of these ladies are as beautiful, healthy, and vibrant as can be. You would never know they'd had serious health challenges and almost died. I have seen many cases like this that looked hopeless—including many where the doctors said there was nothing more they could do—and God did a miracle and turned it around.

In Isaiah 61:7, He said, "Because you got a double dose of trouble . . . your inheritance in the land will be doubled and your joy go on forever" (MSG). He knows how to restore us better than we were before. The Israelites were in slavery for 430 years. As God was delivering them from Egypt, He caused the Egyptians to give them gold, silver, and clothing (Exodus 12:35–36). They didn't look like they had been slaves. For forty years as they wandered, there was not one sick or feeble person among the more than two million Israelites (Psalm 105:37). Their clothes and shoes didn't even wear out (Deuteronomy 29:5). That is supernatural restoration!

You don't have to know when or how God is going to turn your situation around. Your job is to stay in faith and keep a good attitude. Remember, God cares about our needs, but He responds to our faith. Don't complain, get bitter, or lose hope. Give God something to work with in the fire. When you least expect it, your breakthrough will come suddenly, and He will bring you out with the victory!

Father, thank You for being with me in the fire and that You promised in Isaiah 43:1–3 to make me fireproof. Thank You that I will emerge from this healed, victorious, and without even the smell of smoke. I won't look like what I've been through! I praise You because You are a mighty healing, restoring God. In Jesus' name, Amen.

# DAY 13

# A New Perspective

Be renewed in the spirit of your mind.

Ephesians 4:23

Perspective is one of the most powerful forces in life. Our perspective influences how we respond to everything in life. It's the glass-half-empty versus the glass-half-full metaphor. Or the saying, one man's trash is another man's treasure. It's all a matter of perspective. Steven Furtick said, "Your perspective will either become your prison or your passport."[1] When you're battling a serious illness, it can become a daily grind. It's easy to get in a rut where your life becomes consumed by the illness and you're just enduring each day as it comes. If you're going to stay positive and keep your faith strong, you must work to maintain a victorious perspective about your situation. The Scripture says, "Be continually renewed in the spirit of your mind [having a fresh, untarnished mental and spiritual attitude]" (Ephesians 4:23 AMP). Today, I want to encourage you to look at your situation with a new perspective.

Moses sent twelve spies into the Promised Land. All of them saw the same exact thing, yet ten returned and said, "There are giants in the land, and we are like grasshoppers in our own sight. We are not able to overcome those giants." Two of the spies said, "We are well able. Let us go up at once and possess the land." Same situation; two totally different perspectives. One was defeatist and only looking at things in the natural; the other was faith-filled and victorious. Guess which perspective God honored? The two who gave the positive, "can do" report were the only two out of that group of two million Israelites to make it into the Promised Land (Numbers 13).

When Jesus and His disciples were crossing the Sea of Galilee in a boat, a storm suddenly arose. The wind and waves were beating against the boat, and it was taking on water. The disciples were panic-stricken, but Jesus was peacefully asleep in the boat. The disciples woke Jesus and said, "Teacher, do You not care that we are perishing?" Jesus arose, rebuked the wind and waves, and said, "Peace, be still!" Then there was a great calm (Mark 4:35–41). Same situation; two totally different perspectives and responses. God is not worried, fearful, or frustrated. His plans for you are good, and your sickness is no match for Him. Get in sync with His perspective of your situation.

God told Abram, "Lift [up] your eyes now and look from the place where you are . . . for all the land which you see I give to you and your descendants forever" (Genesis 13:14–15). Later, He took Abram outside and told him to look up, that his descendants would be as numerous as the stars (Genesis 15:5). When God made those promises, Abram was 75 years old and had no children. Twice, God told him to look up and gave him a powerful visual to help him get a new perspective. I'm asking you to look up from your current situation, get God's perspective, and have a fresh vision of victory. Sometimes just a slight adjustment in our thinking can suddenly and radically change our perspective for the better. Here are a few thoughts to help shift your perspective today:

- If you are alive, you are better off than 166,324 other people in the world who died today.[2]
- If you have access to good health care, you are better off than four billion people in the world who don't.[3]
- If you have clean water to drink, you are better off than two billion people in the world who don't.[4]
- If you can read this, you are better off than eight hundred million people in the world who can't read.[5]
- No matter what your situation is, there are probably millions (if not billions) of people who are worse off and would gladly trade places with you.

Zoom out and look at your situation with a new perspective. Think about what is right in your life and what you're thankful for instead of what's wrong. Think about what you have instead of what you don't have. When you change how you look at things, the things you look at will begin to change.

Father God, I ask You to renew my mind and give me a fresh, new perspective on my situation. Help me to have a thankful, victorious mindset. In Jesus' name, Amen.

# DAY 14

# The Superpower
# of Gratitude

In everything give thanks; for this is the will of God in Christ
Jesus for you.

1 Thessalonians 5:18

Two of the most powerful words you can ever utter are
"thank you." If you want to attract more of God's
healing power and blessings, develop a habit of thanking Him throughout the day for everything. Thank Him for
what He is doing and has done in your life. Thank Him
by faith for your healing that's on the way. Thank Him for
everything that is right in your life instead of dwelling on
what is wrong. The more you thank God for what is going

right, the more He will take care of what is wrong. There are few things that please God more than a spirit of gratitude.

Everyone likes to be thanked when they do something for someone else. I don't know about you, but the more thankful somebody is, the more I want to do for them. The less thankful they are, the less I want to do for them. The story of the ten lepers Jesus healed in Luke 17 shows that God is the same way. When the ten lepers saw Jesus, "they lifted up their voices and said, 'Jesus, Master, have mercy on us!'" (Luke 17:13). Jesus told them to go and show themselves to the priests, and as they obeyed His instruction, they were miraculously healed. The miracle is often tied to an instruction God gives us. Surprisingly, only one leper bothered to come back and thank Jesus for healing him. It's interesting that they "lifted up their voices" and poured on the charm— calling Him "Master" and begging Him for mercy—when they needed something. But when they got what they were asking for, they took the blessing and ran down the road without even thanking Him for it.

The Bible says one leper "returned, and with a loud voice glorified God, and fell down . . . at His feet, giving Him thanks" (Luke 17:15–16). That's how we should be with God. It's His breath in our lungs. We wouldn't have even woken up today without Him. We would be on our way to hell if it wasn't for His mercy and grace. No matter what you are facing, there are three irrefutable facts: 1) your situation could be worse; 2) there are many people worse off than you who would trade places with you in a heartbeat; and 3) there are many things in your life to be thankful for; not everything is bad in your life! Be like that one leper. Never stop giving thanks.

Jesus asked the thankful leper, "Were there not ten cleansed? But where are the nine? Were there not any found who returned to give glory to God except this foreigner? . . . Arise, go your way. Your faith has made you well" (Luke 17:17–19). It is clear from Jesus' questions that He wanted and expected to be thanked. In the original Greek, the word "well" is the word *sozo*, which means "to save, to make whole in every way." This leper had already been physically healed of leprosy, like the other nine, but he got an extra blessing of wholeness in his entire being because of his thankfulness. Gratitude is a superpower that ushers in God's healing, wholeness, and abundance.

Malachi 3:16 says that God hears everything we say, and our words are recorded in a book of remembrance before God. When God looks up your name in that book of remembrance, don't let Him read about your complaining, negativity, and doubt. Instead, let your name be associated with gratitude and praise. That's what God responds to. In the 25 years I have ministered to sick people, the ones who have gotten miracles all had a thankful spirit.

Philippians 4:6–7 commands us, "Be anxious for nothing, but in everything by prayer and supplication, *with thanksgiving*, let your requests be made known to God; *and the peace of God, which surpasses all understanding, will guard your hearts and minds through Christ Jesus.*" The words "with thanksgiving" were not just thrown in there as an afterthought. When we go to God with our requests, we should always include plenty of thanksgiving. I believe our gratefulness should always outweigh our requests. As we do this, the supernatural peace of God will guard our hearts and minds—another huge blessing of thankfulness.

Father God, thank You for everything You have done, are doing, and will do in my life. I thank You by faith that my healing is on the way. Thank You for giving me the best doctors, nurses, and others involved in my care. Help me always to have a thankful spirit and express my gratitude throughout the day. In Jesus' precious name, Amen.

# Reflections and Prayers

What are your key takeaways from the past seven days?

Based on those takeaways, what action steps could you implement to help your journey to healing?

Use this space to write your current prayer requests to God and anything God has spoken to you about your situation through His Word, the Holy Spirit, people, dreams, or other means.

# DAY 15

## Program Your Mind for Victory

Be very careful about what you think. Your thoughts run your life.

Proverbs 4:23 ICB

Navigating a serious illness can be one of the most grueling battles of the mind anyone ever faces. The "spin cycle" of doctor visits, testing, treatment, hospital stays, deluge of information to process, and often a lack of sleep can be mentally exhausting. Then there are the negative thoughts, fears, questions, lies from the enemy, and sometimes doubts that can attack your mind. If you are going to win the battle for your health, it starts with winning the battle for your mind. Your mind is the control center for your life. You can't think negative, defeated thoughts and have a positive outcome. You can't think *I'll never get well*, or *I may not make it*, and expect to get healed. You draw in what you are thinking about. The enemy knows that if he can get your mind going in the wrong direction, you won't be able to operate in the faith you need to be healed.

Most people have what is called a negativity bias. Our minds tend to go to the negative. This is because for thousands of years, humans were hunters and gatherers. We always had to be on the lookout for saber-toothed tigers and other threats. We had to look out for the negative to survive. So the human brain "evolved" with this built-in negativity bias. This is why there can be a beautiful sunset on the way home from work and people will drive down the highway at 80 miles per hour while talking on the phone, but if there is a wreck, people will almost always slow down to look. This is why bad news sells on the nightly news. If you are like most people, you're not just going to think positive, faith-filled thoughts automatically, especially when you're going through a serious battle for your health. You have to be intentional and determined about thinking the right thoughts.

First Peter 1:13 says to "gird up the loins of your mind." That means to prepare your mind for battle. This is when it matters the most. Your mind is like a powerful supercomputer, and you must program it for victory. Today, I want to give you several effective ways to do this:

1. **Start smart.** How you start each day determines what kind of day you will have. Never start the day passive or in neutral. Begin each day reading the Word of God, praying, declaring Scriptures over yourself, and thanking God for everything that is right in your life. This will set your mind in the right direction at the outset. When you fill your mind with the right thoughts, there won't be room for the wrong thoughts. Proverbs 17:22 says, "A cheerful mind works healing" (AMPC).

2. **Feed your mind a healthy diet.** It's not enough just to have a great devotional time in the morning. Just like you feed your body healthy food throughout the day, you need to feed your mind a healthy diet. Read the Bible or listen to God's Word on audio. Read my book *God Heals* or another inspiring Christian book. Listen to messages that encourage your faith on YouTube or in a podcast, watch Christian television, or listen to praise music.

3. **Tell your mind what to think.** The apostle Paul said, "I think myself happy" (Acts 26:2). You can think yourself afraid, defeated, and depressed, or you can think yourself joyful and victorious. Nobody else can manage your thought life but you. You have to tell your mind what to think. On purpose, you need to go through the day thinking thoughts like *I am healed by the stripes of Jesus. No weapon formed against me shall prosper. I*

*can do all things through Christ who strengthens me. In all things, I am more than a conqueror. God always causes me to triumph. This sickness is no match for my God.*

4. **Reject and replace.** If an intruder got into your house, you wouldn't say, "Have a seat. Make yourself comfortable. Would you like something to drink?" No, you would act quickly and forcefully to remove him. When negative thoughts enter your mind, you have to treat them like an intruder. You can't be passive. You can't meditate on them or agree with them. You must reject them right away and replace them with the right thoughts. Just like you change the channels on the television or swipe to another post on social media, you can change your thoughts.

Heavenly Father, I ask You to set a guard around my mind and protect me from negative thoughts, lies, and wrong beliefs. Help me to program my mind for victory every day and keep my mind going in the right direction. In Jesus' name, Amen.

# DAY 16

# First See It on the Inside

Nothing they have imagined they can do will be impossible for them.

Genesis 11:6 AMPC

In my book *God Heals*, I discussed the extreme importance of faith in the healing process. God cares about our needs, but He responds to our faith. Faith is the currency of heaven, and without it we can't expect to receive anything from God (James 1:6–7). We must believe that we will be healed before our healing will manifest. To help us have the faith we need, God gave us a powerful imagination so we could have an internal visual to which we can attach our faith. He knows we are visual people and that seeing it on the inside helps us believe for it.

Olympic swimmer Michael Phelps, who won an astonishing 23 gold medals (way more than anyone from any sport), used to imagine each race before he swam it. He would imagine himself getting up on the block, doing his trademark arm swings to get loose, bursting off the block for a great start, performing his powerful dolphin kick, swimming smoothly and efficiently, making crisp turns, and steadily pulling ahead until the final sprint, when he reached for the wall and touched it first for the win. Phelps saw himself winning—and he did time after time.[1] In the same way, you must regularly visualize yourself being totally healed and living a long, healthy, vibrant life.

Hebrews 11:3 says, "By faith we understand that the worlds were framed by the word of God, so that *the things which are seen were not made of things which are visible.*" The invisible always precedes the visible. God saw the universe in His mind with invisible thoughts, then He spoke it into existence with invisible words, and then the visible manifested into existence. An architect first sees a building in her mind, then she creates a physical blueprint. What started in her mind then gets built and manifests into physical reality. This is our pattern. *You have to see your healing on the inside before it will ever happen on the outside.*

In Genesis 11:6, God said, "Nothing they have imagined . . . will be impossible for them" (AMPC). That's because our imagination activates our faith, and Jesus said nothing is impossible with faith (Mark 9:23). Unfortunately, the devil knows the power of our imagination, too, and he tries to hijack it with fear and getting us to imagine the worst. The Bible says we have to cast down (reject) these kinds of imaginations, which are contrary to God's Word, and discipline our imagination to spur, not sabotage our faith (2 Corinthians 10:5).

I want to give you two tips that will help you harness the incredible power of your imagination and faith to manifest your healing:

1. Keep pictures around you of happy occasions, when you were healthy, vibrant, and loving life. Imagine yourself being healed and enjoying your life again, like you were in those pictures. This will give you a vision of victory to which you can attach your faith.

2. Imagine what Jesus endured for you to be healed by His stripes, like 1 Peter 2:24 says. He was scourged 39 times by a Roman soldier with a leather whip that had shards of glass and metal tied into it. With every lash, it ripped chunks of flesh out of His back. It was a horrific, bloody scene. They put a crown with long, sharp thorns on His head, which dug deep into His scalp. They nailed Him to the cross by driving long, thick nails into His hands and feet. As He hung there, beaten and battered, they pierced His side with a spear. Jesus suffered mightily to pay the price for your healing (Isaiah 53:4–5 csb; Matthew 8:17; 1 Peter 2:24).

When Tony Meyers imagined Jesus' suffering to pay for his healing, it ignited his faith like never before, and he was miraculously healed of ALS, a supposedly incurable neurological disease. For several years, he had been confined to a wheelchair, barely able to function or speak. One day, as he read an article about Jesus' crucifixion, he said, "I saw Jesus at the whipping post being scourged, and chunks of flesh being ripped off. In His eyes, there was a deep love that was unending. Jesus suffered far worse than me because He loved me that much and wanted me to be whole."[2] There is great power when we remember what Jesus did for us and attach our faith to it!

Father, help me to get a vision on the inside of me being totally healed and living a healthy, wonderful, vibrant life. Help me to have the faith to receive the healing Jesus has already paid for. In Jesus' mighty name, Amen.

# DAY 17

## Conquering Fear

Don't be afraid, for I am with you. Don't be discouraged, for I am your God. I will strengthen you and help you. I will hold you up with my victorious right hand.

Isaiah 41:10 NLT

Fear is one of the biggest challenges people face when battling an illness. There is fear of the unknown, fear of not getting well, fear about how their illness will affect their family, fear of dying, and fears about finances and insurance, to name a few. If you are experiencing fear, it is perfectly normal, but God doesn't want you to stay there. The Bible tells us not to fear 365 times—one for each day of the year. God wants us to resist fear and instead have faith, trust Him, and have His peace, which surpasses all understanding (Philippians 4:7).

Fear is believing that something bad might happen. It's actually having faith for the wrong thing. And since faith is so powerful, fear can cause us to draw in the very thing we fear. Job is a great example. The Bible says he was a "blameless and upright [man] who feared God and shunned evil" (Job 1:1). Because of this, God blessed him with great wealth and a wonderful life (Job 1:2–3). Despite this, Job feared that his sons would mess up somehow, so every morning he rose early and made burnt offerings to God, just in case they sinned (Job 1:5). When Satan came against Job and he lost everything—his family, health, and wealth—Job said, *"The thing I greatly feared has come upon me, and what I dreaded has happened to me"* (Job 3:25). He admitted that his fear of calamity had drawn in the very thing he feared. Fear opens the door to the enemy and trouble. It activates the enemy's power; faith activates God's power.

As believers, we must conquer fear and give it no place in our lives. Instead of being like Job—expecting bad and worrying about what might happen—I'm asking you to expect good. Use your faith to get in agreement with God and manifest His healing promises. Below are three effective strategies for conquering fear that have worked for me and the many people to whom I have ministered:

1. **Soak in God's love.** First John 4:18 says, *"There is no fear in love; but perfect love casts out fear."* When you really understand God's perfect love for you and

allow yourself to receive it, it will cast out all fear from you. When fear rears its ugly head, spend some time meditating on God's love for you. Reread Day 7 in this devotional, entitled "Boundless Love." Receive His love and let it wash over you. Soak in it. As you do this, all your fears, worries, and anxieties will melt away.

2. **Talk back to it.** When Goliath shouted threats at David, David talked back to him. When the devil tempted Jesus in the wilderness, Jesus talked back to him. Three times, He said, "It is written . . . ," quoting the Word of God. Never face the enemy with your mouth closed. When fearful thoughts come, you can't passively sit there and dwell on those thoughts. Open your mouth and say, "God has not given me a spirit of fear, but of power, love, and a sound mind. I reject all fear, anxiety, and worry in the name of Jesus. I receive God's perfect love for me, and His love casts out all fear. I will not fear because God is on the throne and in control. He has me in the palm of His hand."

3. **Take authority over it.** Second Timothy 1:7 says, "God has not given us a *spirit of fear*, but of power and of love and of a sound mind." There is a demonic spirit of fear. I don't believe fear is always caused by a spirit. Sometimes it's our own thoughts and emotions. But often, it's a spirit of fear that is stalking and torment-ing us. When fear comes, say, "I bind, cut off, and cast

out the spirit of fear from me, in Jesus' name. Fear, go now and never come back, in the name of Jesus!" Before I knew about spiritual warfare and my authority in Christ, I used to get horrible panic attacks. I would wake up in the middle of the night feeling like I was having a heart attack and dying. One day, the Lord told me very clearly in my spirit, *That is a spirit. You must take authority over it*. Once I did, the panic attacks stopped, and I've never had one since.

---

Father, thank You that You have not given me a spirit of fear, but of power, love, and a sound mind. Thank You that Your perfect love casts out all fear from me. In Jesus' mighty name, Amen.

# DAY 18

## The Peace of God

You will keep him in perfect peace whose mind is stayed on
You, because he trusts in You.

Isaiah 26:3

The apostle Paul wrote in Philippians 4:6–7, "*Be anxious for nothing*, but in everything by prayer and supplication, with thanksgiving, let your requests be made known to God; *and the peace of God, which surpasses all understanding, will guard your hearts and minds* through Christ Jesus." Paul wrote this while sitting in a Roman prison. His circumstances weren't good. He was in a dark place. Instead of being anxious, Paul tells us to make our petitions known to God through prayer, with thanksgiving. When we use our energy to pray and give God thanks, instead of being anxious, that's when God can fill us with His supernatural peace.

Notice it's the *peace of God*. It comes from God, not the world. Jesus said, "Peace I leave with you, My peace I give to you; not as the world gives do I give to you" (John 14:27). Peace is a fruit of the Holy Spirit, who lives inside us (Galatians 5:22). We have to choose to access this peace. Not doing so is like having ten million dollars in the bank but living like we're in lack. The shoes of peace are one of the pieces of the armor of God Paul writes about in Ephesians 6. Paul tells us to put on the armor. Peace is not something that happens automatically. We have to purposely put on peace. Paul based this passage on the armor worn by Roman soldiers. Their shoes had spikes on the bottom so they could dig into the ground and hold their position. We have to dig our shoes of peace in and refuse to let anything move us out of our peace. Peace is power.

Paul describes God's peace as surpassing all understanding. That means it makes no sense in the natural. When other people succumb to fear and discouragement, you can have God's divine, unshakable peace, knowing that He is on the throne and in control, He has you in the palm of His hand, and He has the best plan for your life. Paul finishes the verse by saying that God's peace will guard your heart and mind through Christ Jesus. In the Greek, this is military verbiage that means it will protect your heart and mind like a heavily guarded castle. This happens "through

Christ Jesus." It's not our own ability, but the intervention of Jesus that allows us to have this peace. He is the Prince of Peace (Isaiah 9:6).

Dr. Ryan Hall, a transplant surgeon in Houston, shared a poignant story about a patient of his who demonstrated this peace that surpasses all understanding. He said when he saw this patient a year before, there was a tumor taking up half his liver and its location prevented him from removing it. To make matters worse, the biopsy showed this was the worst kind of liver cancer, one that does not respond well to chemotherapy and from which people usually die within six months. Dr. Hall walked into the room expecting to see an emaciated, jaundiced man barely clinging to life. He said,

> I found a man who looked as healthy as me. Wearing his reflective vest, he was heading to work after this appointment. His baseball cap said something like, "If you need answers, read the instructions," and had a Bible on it. Thrilled to see him doing so well, I asked how he was doing. He said, "Oh, the cancer? (like it was an afterthought). It shrank some and hasn't grown any. It's not my problem." My stunned expression prompted him to elaborate. He said in a quieter voice, "I gave my whole life to Jesus." Then he held out his hands in front of him, palms up, and said, "My *whole* life. So no matter what happens, it's not my problem. I get up at 4:30 every morning, get on the treadmill or bike, lift weights, then go to work to provide for my family." In the end, I felt like that appointment was for me. That man had unshakable

peace and trust in God. There was no fear or despair whatsoever in his demeanor. Just peace that can only come from God. I left with a greater understanding of what it means to give my *whole* life to Jesus and receive His divine peace that transcends circumstances.

Just like this patient, you can choose to be anxious for nothing. Let the peace of God, which surpasses all understanding, guard your heart and mind. Every day, put on your shoes of peace and refuse to be moved out of your peace for any reason.

Heavenly Father, thank You for your supernatural peace, which guards my heart and mind through Christ Jesus. In Jesus' name, Amen.

# DAY 19

# It Is Well

It is well.

2 Kings 4:26

In the Old Testament, there was a woman who gave the prophet Elisha a place to stay and meals to eat whenever he was in her city (2 Kings 4:8–37). One day, Elisha asked what he could do to repay her kindness. The woman said she wanted a son, but she was barren and her husband was old. Elisha promised her that by that time the next year, she would embrace her son. She gave birth to this child at the appointed time. Years later, the boy was out in the field with his father when he had something like a brain aneurysm or a stroke. He died a short time later. With incredible faith and poise in the midst of tragedy, the mother decided to go find Elisha. When her husband asked what she was doing, she simply replied, "It is well" (2 Kings 4:23). Elisha saw her approaching from a distance and sent his servant to check on her. She told the servant, "It is well" (2 Kings 4:26). When they returned to her dead son, he prayed over him with Elisha's staff, but nothing happened. Then she appealed directly to Elisha, and when he prayed and lay on top of the dead boy, the boy miraculously came back to life!

I want to meet this amazing woman when I get to heaven. What a fearless heroine of the faith! She started off with a big, bold ask, believing the prophet could give her a baby as a barren, elderly woman. Then, when the boy tragically died, she was undaunted and, once again, displayed audacious faith. Twice, she declared out of her mouth, "It is well," and believed that God could use the prophet to resurrect her son. Because of her big, tenacious faith, she got a double miracle. Be an "It is well" person, like this lady. There is nothing our God can't do. Dare to believe Him for your miracle, no matter what the doctor's report is or what it looks like in the natural.

Another "It is well" person was Horatio Spafford, who wrote the poignant, beloved church hymn "It Is Well with My Soul" in 1873. Spafford was not a songwriter but a wealthy attorney and Presbyterian church leader. He lived in Chicago with his wife and five children. Life was great until 1871, when the Great Fire of Chicago devastated the city and reduced Spafford's properties to ashes. Two years later,

Spafford decided to take a much-needed vacation with his family in England. He got delayed because of business, so he sent his wife and four daughters ahead. While crossing the Atlantic on the steamship, their vessel was struck by another ship. Two hundred and twenty-six people perished, including all four of Spafford's daughters. Remarkably, his wife survived and sent him a telegram that said simply, "Saved alone. . . ." Receiving her message, Spafford immediately left on a ship to meet up with his wife in England. One day during the voyage, the captain summoned him and told him that according to his charts, they were at the spot where his daughters had died. Spafford returned to his cabin and wrote the hymn "It Is Well with My Soul."[1] Because he chose to trust God and refused to give in to self-pity or anger, God has used the words Spafford wrote that day to impact millions of lives all over the world.

Holocaust survivor Corrie ten Boom said, "When a train goes through a tunnel and it gets dark, you don't throw away the ticket and jump off. You sit still and trust the engineer."[2] No matter what twists and turns your healing journey takes, what disappointments and setbacks you may encounter, or how dark it gets at times, you can trust your Engineer. Even when you don't see anything happening or things are going in the wrong direction, God is working in the unseen realm. Jesus said, "My Father is always working" (John 5:17 NLT). He is on the throne and in control. He has you in the palm of His hand. He has a great plan for your life. He is in you, with you, and for you. He will never leave nor forsake you. Have faith for your healing, pray bold prayers, and declare the Word of God over yourself daily, then trust God with the rest. Pass the test. It is well, and everything is going to be okay.

---

Father God, thank You that it is well with me because You are on the throne and have me in the palm of Your hand. I trust You to heal me and bring me out with the victory at the appointed time. In Jesus' name, Amen.

# DAY 20

# Rejoice!

Rejoice in the Lord always. Again I will say, rejoice!

Philippians 4:4

When Paul wrote the above verse, he was sitting in a smelly, hot, dark Roman prison. He wasn't imprisoned for any real crime but for doing the very thing God called him to do—preaching the gospel. He had little reason in the natural to rejoice. Yet Paul said to rejoice in the Lord always and even repeated it for emphasis—"Again I will say, rejoice!" In 1 Thessalonians 5:16, 18, he wrote, "Rejoice always . . . for this is the will of God in Christ Jesus for you." Why? What was Paul trying to tell us between the lines? I suppose it was the same thing

David was trying to convey in Psalm 118:24: "This is the day the LORD has made; we will rejoice and be glad in it."

David had many tough trials, and in the earlier part of this psalm he wrote, "All nations surrounded me. . . . They surrounded me like bees. . . . [My enemies] pushed me violently, that I might fall" (Psalm 118:10, 12, 13). Like Paul, David was saying, *My circumstances might not be good, but God is good all the time. He woke me up this morning. He gave me breath to breathe. He's been good to me my whole life. This is the day He has made, and I choose as an act of my will to rejoice and be glad in it.*

Peter and the apostles were beaten by the Jewish religious leaders for preaching the gospel. Instead of being despondent and thinking, *How could God let us go through this?* the Bible says, "The apostles left the high council *rejoicing* that God had counted them worthy to suffer disgrace for the name of Jesus" (Acts 5:41 NLT).

The prophet Habakkuk wrote, "Though the fig tree may not blossom, nor fruit be on the vines; though the labor of the olive may fail, and the fields yield no food; though the flock may be cut off from the fold, and there be no herd in the stalls—yet I will *rejoice* in the LORD, I will *joy* in the God of my salvation" (Habakkuk 3:17–18).

How is it possible that Paul wrote about rejoicing in the Lord while sitting in prison, David rejoiced in the Lord while he was surrounded by his enemies, Peter and the apostles rejoiced after being beaten, and Habakkuk rejoiced after the bottom fell out of his finances? What did they know that we can learn from?

The word *rejoice* in all these verses means to find joy in the Lord despite adverse circumstances. These people of faith learned to get their joy from the Lord alone instead of the shifting sands of circumstances. Nehemiah 8:10 says, "The joy of the LORD is your strength." Despair is weakness; joy is strength. The joy of the Lord will give you the strength you need to win the battle for your health.

A hospital chaplain friend of mine told me about a 34-year-old woman with children who had both her lungs destroyed by COVID and needed a double lung transplant. She was on the transplant list for around 650 days. She lived in the hospital continuously for 345 days. Can you imagine? But everyone who went into her room said she always had a joyful countenance. She always had a smile on her face and radiated Jesus. This woman rejoiced in the Lord daily and tapped in to the supernatural joy of the Lord, which doesn't depend on circumstances. She eventually got two brand-new lungs and is healthy and thriving today.

Here's my encouragement to you. No matter what you are facing:

Reject discouragement.
Reject negativity.
Reject fear.
Reject doubt.

Reject self-pity.

Reject frustration.

Reject worry.

Instead, rejoice in the Lord your God!

Rejoice that your name is written in the Lamb's Book of Life and nothing can take that away from you (Luke 10:20; Revelation 21:27; John 10:28).

Rejoice that you are God's beloved child (1 John 3:1; John 1:12; Romans 8:16).

Rejoice that God passionately and unconditionally loves, approves of, and accepts you (1 John 3:1; Romans 5:8; 1 John 4:9–10; Ephesians 1:6).

Rejoice that nothing can separate you from God's love (Romans 8:38–39).

Rejoice that God will never leave you, nor forsake you (Deuteronomy 31:8; Hebrews 13:5).

Rejoice that you are healed by the stripes of Jesus and it's just a matter of time before your healing manifests (Isaiah 53:4–5 CSB; Matthew 8:17; 1 Peter 2:24).

Rejoice that no weapon formed against you shall prosper (Isaiah 54:17).

Rejoice that God always leads you to triumph in Christ Jesus (2 Corinthians 2:14).

Father God, I choose as an act of my will to rejoice in You. Fill me with Your supernatural joy, which is my strength, and help me to win the battle for my health. In Jesus' name, Amen.

# DAY 21

# One Thing Is Needed

One thing is needed.

Luke 10:42

As I have ministered to thousands of sick people and their families over the years, I have observed how all-consuming a serious illness can be. There is the "spin cycle" of endless doctor visits, tests, treatments, and hospital stays. There are concerns about family, finances, insurance coverage, and many other things. In the torrent of earthly cares, your daily fellowship with God can fall by the wayside if you're not careful. Today, I hope to refocus and refire you about the one thing Jesus said is needed most:

Now it happened as they went that He entered a certain village; and a certain woman named Martha welcomed Him into her house. And she had a sister called Mary, who also *sat at Jesus' feet and heard His word.* But Martha was *distracted* with much serving, and she approached Him and said, "Lord, do You not care that my sister has left me to serve alone? Therefore tell her to help me."

And Jesus answered and said to her, "Martha, Martha, you are worried and troubled about many things. But one thing is needed, and Mary has chosen that good part, which will not be taken away from her."

Luke 10:38–42

Martha was so distracted that she didn't even fellowship with Jesus when He was in her home. He said, "Martha, Martha, you are worried and troubled about many things." You may be worried and troubled about many things, too. But Jesus said that *one thing is needed.* Not two, three, or five things. *One thing.* No matter what trial or chaos you are walking through, one thing is needed. What was the one thing Jesus was talking about? Mary was fellowshiping with Jesus and listening to Him. Everything you need—hope, faith, strength, grace, encouragement, healing, and more—flows out of this one thing: your daily fellowship with Jesus.

In John 15, Jesus said, "Abide in Me, and I in you. . . . I am the vine, you are the branches. . . . Without Me you can do nothing. . . . If you abide in Me, and My words abide in you, you will ask what you desire, and it shall be done for you" (John 15:4–5, 7). Jesus used the word *abide* seven times in this passage. Nowhere else in the Bible is a word repeated seven times in one passage. That's how important abiding is to Jesus. The word *abide* means to remain in continuous fellowship with Jesus—not just on Sunday morning or during our morning "quiet time," but throughout the day. Jesus said that He is the Vine and we are the branches. Branches get their nourishment and strength from the vine. When a branch becomes disconnected from the vine, it quickly weakens and withers. That is a picture of us when we become disconnected from daily fellowship with Jesus. But notice the incredible promise Jesus attached to abiding: you can ask whatever you desire, and it will be done for you. The pathway to healing and whatever else you desire starts with abiding in Christ and keeping Him first place in your life.

My friend Austin was miraculously healed of stage 4 metastatic liver cancer that four top doctors deemed "terminal." I shared his testimony in Day 1 of this devotional. Below, he describes in his own words how abiding in Christ helped him receive his miracle:

> While fighting terminal cancer, my wife and I did everything we could to abide in Christ. That meant keeping our minds filled with God-centered thoughts so there wasn't room for negative, defeated thoughts. When negative thoughts came—which was often—I would say out loud, "Get behind me, Satan" (Matthew 4:10) and say several Scriptures on healing. When I woke up every morning, I started by thanking God for another day of life and then went straight to reading the Word of God to set my mind in the right

direction. Throughout the day, I kept my mind focused on God by listening to praise music and anointed sermons online. I kept note cards with Bible verses on my desk, in my closet, in the bathroom, and in the kitchen. This effort was far beyond "positive thinking." It was speaking the truth, the very Word of God, over my situation. God uses His Word to heal (Psalm 107:20), and we are called to take every thought captive to the obedience of Christ (2 Corinthians 10:5). Life is so much better when we live in and for Jesus.

Father, no matter what is going on in my life, help me to keep You in first place and abide in Christ throughout the day, for this is the path to healing and victory. In Jesus' name, Amen.

# Reflections and Prayers

What are your key takeaways from the past seven days?

_____

_____

_____

_____

_____

Based on those takeaways, what action steps could you implement to help your journey to healing?

_____

_____

_____

_____

_____

Use this space to write your current prayer requests to God and anything God has spoken to you about your situation through His Word, the Holy Spirit, people, dreams, or other means.

# DAY 22

## Prayer Power

The earnest (heartfelt, continued) prayer of a righteous man
makes tremendous power available.

James 5:16 AMPC

According to the above verse, your prayers make God's unlimited power available. Prayer is our spiritual lifeblood that connects us to the Source of everything we need. It's not only the most important way we have fellowship and intimacy with God, but it gives Him permission to move in our lives. That's why the apostle Paul said to "pray without ceasing" and "pray in the Spirit on all occasions with all kinds of prayers and requests" (1 Thessalonians 5:17; Ephesians 6:18 NIV). In other words, pray about everything all the time. Don't just pray for healing. Pray for wisdom and guidance about every health-care decision. Pray about every test and procedure. Pray for your doctors and health-care workers. Pray about your finances. Pray about small things, like a good parking spot. God knows the number of hairs on our head, so nothing is too trivial for Him. He wants to be involved in every aspect of our lives. The God of the universe hears your prayers, and they are powerful!

God added fifteen more years to Hezekiah's life when he prayed (Isaiah 38:2, 4–5). God delivered Jonah from the belly of a fish when he prayed (Jonah 2:1). When Peter was in prison, God sent an angel to free him when the church prayed (Acts 12:5–10). Paul and Silas prayed and sang hymns at midnight in a Roman prison, and God sent an earthquake that freed every prisoner. Even the jailer and his family got saved (Acts 16:25–34)! Peter prayed, and a woman was raised from the dead (Acts 9:36–42). Elijah prayed, and a boy was raised from the dead (1 Kings 17:21–22). These stories are in the Bible not so we can idolize these people, but as examples for us. They were not superhuman, but they had flaws, weaknesses, and struggles just like we do. I want to share a few keys that will help your prayers produce supernatural results like theirs!

1. **Pray with confidence and boldness**. The enemy wants you to think, *Who do you think you are? You know what you did. Why would God answer your prayers?* He doesn't want you to pray with confidence and ex-

pectancy. If you are going to pray powerful prayers that get results, you must reject lies and limiting thoughts. All have sinned and fallen short of God's glory, but we have been forgiven, cleansed of all unrighteousness, and made worthy by the blood of Jesus. The Bible says, "We have *confidence* to enter the Most Holy Place by the blood of Jesus," and it beckons us to "come *boldly* to the throne of grace" (Hebrews 10:19 NIV; Hebrews 4:16). Don't pray insecure, "I'm not worthy" prayers. Pray with confidence and boldness as a blood-bought, blood-washed child of the Most High God and heir of His Kingdom.

2. **Pray with faith.** Praying to God with religious formality, Elizabethan English, or flowery eloquence doesn't impress God or move Him to act. He is your Abba, Daddy. He wants you to be yourself and pray with intimacy and sincerity. What moves God to act is faith. Jesus said, "Whatever things you ask in prayer, *believing*, you will receive" (Matthew 21:22). The key is to believe in what you are praying for. The Scripture says that if we believe, all things are possible, but without faith we can't receive anything from God (Mark 9:23; James 1:6–7). Faith is the X factor for prayers that get results.

3. **Pray the solution, not the problem.** Praying complaining-type prayers and rehearsing the problem with God may

make your flesh feel good, but it accomplishes nothing. The most effective way to pray is to quote God's Word back to Him in your prayers. His Word is His covenant with us and the only thing He is bound to. By praying God's Word back to Him in faith, you are agreeing with His promises and giving them permission to manifest in your life. God watches over His Word to perform it (Jeremiah 1:12 NASB).

4. **Have patience and persistence.** The Scripture says it is by faith *and* patience that we inherit the promises of God (Hebrews 6:12). We need both. God doesn't work like a drive-through window. He has His own timetable and agenda. Jesus taught that we need to be like the persistent widow and "at all times . . . pray and not give up and lose heart" (Luke 18:1 AMP).

5. **Forgive.** Jesus said, "Whenever you stand *praying*, if you have anything against anyone, forgive him" (Mark 11:25). Get rid of all unforgiveness, anger, grudges, and strife. These things will hinder your prayers.

Father, thank You that my prayers make Your unlimited power available for healing and every need I have. In Jesus' name, Amen.

# DAY 23

# Open Your Mouth

Death and life are in the power of the tongue.

Proverbs 18:21

Your mouth is one of the most powerful weapons you have in the battle to reclaim your health. Its importance cannot be overemphasized or exaggerated. I have seen countless miracle healings, and in virtually every case, the person or someone in their circle knew how to wield the power of their mouth. With your mouth, you declare God's Word over yourself, pray, praise God, and exercise your authority over the enemy—all indispensable components of winning the battle for your health. The enemy would love for you to passively sit there and "suffer in silence," but the path to victory is to open your mouth throughout the day and strategically direct its awesome power. Today, I want to focus on the importance and power of using your mouth to relentlessly declare God's Word over yourself and your situation.

Hebrews 4:12 (AMP) says, "The word of God is *living* and *active* and *full of power*." First, the Word is *living*. Second Timothy 3:16 (NIV) says, "All Scripture is God-breathed." He literally breathed the same life-giving breath that created humankind from the dust of the ground into His written Word and infused it with life and supernatural power. You can't say that about any other written words. Second, God's Word is *active*. It's not passive. It's not neutral. When you speak it over your health, body, life, and situation, it *goes to work*. In Jeremiah 1:12 (ESV), God said, "I am watching over my word to *perform it*." When you declare out loud specific Scriptures that apply to your situation, the God of the universe watches over it to perform the promises contained in those Scriptures. And because it is performed by the most powerful force in the universe, it is full of supernatural, wonder-working power.

God said, "He who has My word, let him speak My word faithfully. . . . Is not My word like a fire . . . and like a hammer that breaks the rock in pieces?" (Jeremiah 23:28–29). God's Word is like a fire that consumes sickness, disease, cancer, viruses, and infections. It's like a hammer that breaks tumors, blockages, and aneurysms into pieces. But we must do the first part of the verse and *speak His Word faithfully*. Find some healing Scriptures in God's Word and declare them over yourself daily. By doing this, you are agreeing with it and giving it permission to come to pass. When you make these declarations several times a day, they will get down in your spirit, and you will start believing them. Your faith will rise, and you will live with expectancy about receiving the promises of God. They will also renew your mind, so you are able to resist negative thoughts, fear, doubt, and discouragement. There is a miracle in your mouth when you regularly declare God's Word over yourself!

This does not work like a magic wand, where you get immediate results every time. You have to make these declarations with persistence, determination, and faith. Here are a few declarations to get you started:

- God is my Healer, and He will restore me to perfect health (Exodus 15:26; 23:25; Jeremiah 30:17).
- Jesus bore my sicknesses and pains upon Himself at the cross, and by His stripes I am healed (Matthew 8:17; 1 Peter 2:24).
- God heals all my diseases (Psalm 103:2–3).
- God has heard my prayer and seen my tears; *surely* He will heal me (2 Kings 20:5).
- God will restore health to me and heal all my wounds (Jeremiah 30:17).
- God is healing my blood and every cell, organ, gland, tissue, muscle, ligament, tendon, and bone in my body.

- The same Spirit who raised Jesus from the dead dwells in me and gives life, energy, vim, vigor, vitality, and strength to my mortal body (Romans 8:11).
- With long life God will satisfy me and show me His deliverance (Psalm 91:16).
- I will not die but live to declare the works of the Lord (Psalm 118:17).
- No weapon formed against me shall prosper (Isaiah 54:17).
- In all things, I am more than a conqueror (Romans 8:37).
- God always causes me to triumph in Christ Jesus (2 Corinthians 2:14; 1 Corinthians 15:57).

Father, thank You for Your Word, which is living, active, and full of wonder-working power! It is like a fire that burns away sickness and like a hammer that breaks rocks into pieces. Help me to regularly and relentlessly declare Your Word over myself and my situation. As I do, I thank You that You will watch over Your Word to perform it in my life. In Jesus' mighty name, Amen.

# DAY 24

# Whatever You Say

He will have whatever he says.

Mark 11:23

God created the universe by the words of His mouth. He simply said, "Let there be . . ." and everything was created out of nothing. The Bible says He created us in His image and likeness, and He gave our words the same kind of power. Proverbs 18:21 says, "Death and life are in the power of the tongue." There is no greater power on earth than the power of life and death, and yet God Himself put that power in our mouth. Our words can produce either healing, life, and victory or sickness, death, and defeat. So we must wield its power wisely.

Jesus reinforced the incredible power of our words when He said in Mark 11:23, "Whoever says to this mountain, 'Be removed and be cast into the sea,' and does not doubt in his heart, but believes that those things he says will be done, *he will have whatever he says.*" I want you to say that last phrase out loud three times to get it down in your spirit:

"He will have whatever he says."

"He will have whatever he says."

"He will have whatever he says."

*Whatever* means both positive or negative, so make sure you are strategic about your words and only speak what you want to see manifested. Job 22:28 says, "You will also declare a thing, and it will be established for you." This theme of the power of our words and our ability to declare things and see them come to pass is repeated throughout the Bible. You can't speak sickness and have health. You can't speak defeat and have victory. You can't have a negative, complaining, whiny mouth and have a positive life. You can't speak poverty and lack and have prosperity. Your life is going to follow your words. Joel 3:10 says, "Let the weak say, 'I am strong.'" Not "Let the weak say, 'I am weak.'" Don't use your words to describe your situation; use your words to *change* your situation.

Notice in the verse above from Mark 11:23, Jesus didn't say to talk *about* the mountain or complain to our family and friends about the mountain. He told us to *speak to* the mountain. He said if we don't doubt in our heart—if our words are mixed with faith—we could command mountains to be removed and have whatever things we say. Faith gives substance to and brings into manifestation the words we speak. Your "mountain" is your medical condition or anything else that stands between you and the promises of God. Jesus gives us one of the most effective strategies for healing: speak directly to your sickness or condition out loud and *command* it to go from your body in Jesus' name. Do it with faith, do it with authority, and do it often.

My favorite healing story in the Bible is about the woman with the issue of blood in Mark 5:25–34. She had a dreadful bleeding condition for twelve years and had spent all her money on doctors, only to get worse. But she never lost faith. She was determined to be healed if it was the last thing she did. She kept saying to herself, *If I can only touch the hem of His garment, I know I will be made well.*[1] And that is exactly what happened! Her own faith-filled words finally manifested into reality.

Below are some declarations I encourage you to make over yourself one or more times a day:

- The healing power of God is flowing through my body and permeating every cell in my body. My blood, immune system, bone marrow, and every cell, organ, gland, tissue, bone, muscle, ligament, and tendon in my body is healthy and whole, and it functions the way God designed it to function.

- Jesus said in Mark 11:23 that I can command a mountain to be removed and if I don't doubt in my heart, I can have whatever things I say. So in the name of Jesus, I command every sickness, disease, pain, and symptom to go from my body. I command healing, wholeness, and restoration to every cell in my body, in Jesus' mighty name.

---

Father, thank You for the awesome power You have put in my mouth. Help me to wield the power of my words wisely. In Jesus' precious name, Amen.

# DAY 25

# Guard against Negative Words

Now He did not do many mighty works there because of their unbelief.

Matthew 13:58

In the previous two days, I discussed the power of declaring God's Word over yourself and using your own words to foster your healing. Today, I want to cover the importance of protecting you or your loved one from negative words spoken by others. Negative words in the context of healing mainly include words of doubt and unbelief, complaining, talking about the problem, and repeating negative reports from the doctor. There are three compelling reasons you want to avoid negative words like the plague:

1. **Words are incredibly powerful.** Proverbs 18:21 says,
   "Death and life are in the power of the tongue." Outside of God, I can't think of a greater power than death
   and life—and yet God has imbued our own tongue
   with this power. We can speak life or death over ourselves and our situation. Other people's words have
   this power, too, so we have to guard not only against
   ourselves but also against others speaking words that
   could undermine our healing.

   In my book *God Heals*, I talked about creating a
   "faith cocoon" in your home or hospital room, where
   you don't allow people to speak doubt and defeat
   around you or your loved one. When my mother-in-
   law got sepsis in her seventies and all her organs were
   failing, doctors gave a grim prognosis. Certain family
   members started speaking words of death in her room,
   even talking about the need to plan her funeral. My wife
   and I put a stop to that real fast. We lovingly but firmly
   asked them not to speak anything but faith, and if they
   couldn't, to please not come. We spoke life and healing Scriptures over her relentlessly for two weeks. She
   walked out of that hospital completely healed without
   even needing rehab. The doctor called her his "miracle
   patient." I have no doubt she would not have made it
   if we had allowed those negative words to continue.

   If a doctor gives you or your loved one a negative
   report, when they leave your presence say, "I break,

cancel, and nullify the power of every negative word [doctor's name] or anyone else has spoken over me/ [name of your loved one], in Jesus' name. I command every negative word and report to fall to the ground and have no effect, in the mighty name of Jesus. I declare that I/[name of your loved one] am/is healed by the stripes of Jesus. No weapon formed against me/ him/her will prosper."

2. **God will not operate in an atmosphere of unbelief.** Matthew 13:58 says that Jesus did not do many mighty works in His hometown of Nazareth because of their unbelief. Even though God has all power, He chooses to operate only by faith. Faith is the currency of heaven, and He will not do much in an atmosphere of doubt and unbelief. The primary way people express doubt and unbelief is by their *words*.

When God delivered the Israelites from slavery in Egypt, they were a complaining, whiny bunch. God did amazing miracles, even parting the Red Sea, to set them free, but when they got a little way into the wilderness, they started complaining about everything. They even said they wished God had left them as slaves in Egypt (Exodus 16:3)! Finally, God told Moses that He heard their complaints and would do the very things to them He heard them say. He added that none of them would make it into the Promised Land except Joshua and Caleb, who believed God and spoke faith

(Numbers 14:27–30). So take a lesson from the Israelites and watch your mouth! Speak life, faith, praise,
thanksgiving, and victory, and create an atmosphere
that attracts the presence and healing power of God.

3. **Negative words can dampen you or your loved one's
faith and crush your/their spirit.** Proverbs 18:14 says,
"The spirit of a man will sustain him in sickness, but
who can bear a broken spirit?" You want words of faith
and victory going into you or your loved one's spirit,
not words that are going to crush your/their spirit and
hope. Don't grandstand or preach to doctors, but if
your loved one is unconscious, ask the doctor if they
can speak with you about their condition outside the
room, where they can't hear. Unconscious people can
hear every word spoken in their presence, and those
words will affect their spirit.

Father God, I repent for any negative words I have spoken and ask You to break the power of those words and
any negative words that others have spoken over me.
Put a guard around my mouth and help me to only speak
life, faith, and victory. In Jesus' name, Amen.

# DAY 26

## Faith over Feelings

The just shall live by faith.

Hebrews 10:38

Many people have told me their healing journey feels like a roller coaster—and their emotions are along for the ride. They feel the whole range of emotions from happy and hopeful at times to afraid, discouraged, and sad at others. God gave us emotions, but the key is not to let them control us. That's letting the tail wag the dog. If you're going to win the battle for your health, your faith must be stronger than your feelings.

Too many people are controlled by their feelings. They let their feelings decide what kind of day it's going to be. If they feel bad physically or discouraged, it's going to be a bad day. If they feel good physically or positive, it's going to be a good day. But feelings are fickle. They can change on a dime. One minute, we can feel down and hopeless; the next minute, we can get some good news or an uplifting visit and instantly feel positive again. By contract, faith is based on what we know from God's Word rather than how we feel. Faith is believing what we can't feel or see. It is the *opposite* of being controlled by our feelings. We serve a faith God. God cares about our feelings, but He responds to our faith. Every minute we cater to our feelings is a minute we are not operating in faith.

Feelings also can't be trusted. They are poor indicators of the truth. We feel many things that aren't necessarily true or don't line up with the Word of God. Feelings will say you're not going to make it, but God says you will live and not die (Psalm 118:17). Feelings will say you are a victim, but God says you are more than a conqueror (Romans 8:37). Feelings will say God has forsaken you, but God says He will never leave you, nor forsake you (Hebrews 13:5). Feelings will say it's hopeless, but God says all things are possible with Him (Matthew 19:26). If we are going to walk in victory, we must learn to live beyond our feelings.

When David wrote, "This is the day the LORD has made; we will rejoice and be glad in it" (Psalm 118:24), his situation was not good. He was running from Saul, who was trying to kill him, and living in caves. He was saying, "I am going to rule over my feelings. I am going to choose as an act of my will to stay in faith and be positive no matter what my circumstances are." Wake up every morning and *decide* what kind of day you are going to have. Don't let your feelings decide. The Bible says, "Joy comes in the morning" (Psalm 30:5). Discouragement, negativity, and self-pity also come in the morning. You must choose which you are going to receive. When you open your eyes in the morning, say, "Father, I thank You for the breath in my lungs. Thank You that it's going to be a great day and my healing is on the way. Thank You that You always cause me to triumph in Christ Jesus."

Gideon, a judge who ruled over Israel in the Old Testament, struggled with fear and insecurity. He threshed wheat inside a winepress instead of out in the open because he was afraid of the Midianites. An angel appeared to him and said, "The LORD is with you, you mighty man of valor!" (Judges 6:12). Gideon felt like the opposite of a mighty man of valor. He told the angel, "My clan is the weakest in Manasseh, and I am the least in my father's house" (Judges 6:15). But the angel assured him that God was with him and would give him victory over the Midianites. It wasn't easy, but Gideon chose to believe God over his feelings, and God used him mightily. Because he chose faith over feelings, he is regarded as the greatest judge who ruled Israel.

The apostle Paul wrote to the Corinthians, "I was with you in *weakness*, in *fear*, and *in much trembling*. And my speech and my preaching were not with persuasive words of human wisdom, but in demonstration of the Spirit and of power" (1 Corinthians 2:3–4). All the great people in the Bible felt the same things we feel—even Jesus. They had moments of intense fear, discouragement, sadness, and all the other emotions we feel. Paul admitted to feeling weak and afraid with much trembling, but he didn't let his feelings control him. He still walked in the Spirit and power of God. Like David and Gideon, God used Paul greatly, and he is still impacting lives today because he chose faith over feelings.

Heavenly Father, help me to choose faith over feelings every day and not allow my feelings to control me. In Jesus' name, Amen.

# DAY 27

## Faith in the Middle

We walk by faith, not by sight.

2 Corinthians 5:7

When a woman gets pregnant, there is great excitement and celebration at the beginning. There is also great excitement and anticipation when the baby is about to be born. But in the middle, there are nine months during which the mother endures some discomfort and what feels like endless waiting. I remember my wife felt hot all the time when she was pregnant. She would turn the thermostat down to sixty. I would have five blankets on and could see my own breath. Her back would hurt, sometimes her legs swelled, and especially in the last trimester, it was hard for her to get comfortable when she slept. But when that glorious birthday came, it was all worth it!

When you first get diagnosed, it's easy to have faith for your healing. It's also easy to have faith when you can see your healing manifesting and the finish line is in sight. The real challenge is in the middle, when it's taking longer than you thought, when the doctor's reports aren't getting better, and when you don't know what God is up to. That's when you will be tested. God never said that His promises would be fulfilled in our lives without any opposition, setbacks, and things we don't understand. If you are going to win the battle for your health, you must have faith in the middle.

Faith is in the unseen realm. If you can see it or figure it out, you don't need faith. Faith is when you don't see anything happening and it looks impossible in the natural, but you keep standing on the promises of God and trusting Him. Even when doctors and medicine run out of options, God never runs out of options. He can make a way where there seems to be no way. It may look like that condition is permanent. It may look like it's too late. It may look hopeless in the natural, but we serve a supernatural God. Nothing is impossible with Him!

When things aren't happening on your timetable, it looks like it's getting worse in the natural, and lies are bombarding your mind telling you, *It's over; God doesn't care about you; if God was going to heal you, He would have done it by now*, that's when you have to dig deep and stir up that bulldog, never-say-die faith. No matter what it looks like, God is still on the throne. He loves you and has a great plan for your life. This sickness didn't come as a surprise to Him. He's not sitting up in heaven scratching His head worrying about what He's going to do. He will keep His promises and bring you out with the victory if you stay in faith and pass the test of the middle.

God is always at work, even when we are waiting in the middle and it looks like He's not doing anything. Jesus said, "My Father is always working" (John 5:17 NLT). If He wasn't at work, that sickness would have taken you out already. You wouldn't have been able to withstand all the challenges. His mercy, grace, and protection have kept you. Just because your ultimate victory hasn't come yet, don't think God isn't doing anything. He's at work in the unseen realm. If you're not dead, God's not done. If you still have breath in your lungs, God still has a purpose for your life. If He was done with you, He would have taken you home. You're in the middle period, but one touch from God can turn everything around. Your story doesn't end in defeat. Healing, restoration, and victory are on the way!

We don't go from mountaintop to mountaintop in life. In between the mountaintops is a valley. That's the middle ground. Interestingly, not much grows on mountaintops. The valley is where all the growth is. That is the lushest, most fruitful place. We learn and grow the most in the valleys of life. In Psalm 23:4, David wrote, "Yea, though I walk *through* the valley of the shadow of death, I will fear no evil; for *You are with me*; Your rod and Your staff, they comfort me." The word *through* is key. You're not going to stay in this valley. God is with you, and He's going to help you through victoriously. The next verse says, "You prepare a table before me in the presence of my enemies" (Psalm 23:5). On the other side of this valley, God has prepared a table for you. It's a table of healing, victory, joy, and abundant life. Isaiah 3:10 says, "Say to the righteous that it shall be well with them." If you are a believer in Christ, you are one of the righteous, and *it shall be well with you!*

Heavenly Father, help me to stay in faith, keep trusting You, and pass the test of the middle. In Jesus' name, Amen.

# DAY 28

# "I Still Believe" Faith

*Martha:* Lord, if You had been with us, my brother would not have died. Even so *I still believe* that anything You ask of God will be done.
*Jesus:* Your brother will rise to life.

John 11:21–23 VOICE

After Jesus' friend Lazarus died and had already been in the tomb four days, his sisters, Martha and Mary, were so disappointed that Jesus did not come sooner. Martha told Jesus if He had come sooner, Lazarus wouldn't have died. But the next thing she said was a display of astonishing faith. She said, "Even so *I still believe* that anything You ask of God will be done" (VOICE). Can you imagine the kind of faith it took to believe Jesus could resurrect her brother after he'd been dead four days? I pray for you to have some of Martha's "I still believe" faith.

You may have been waiting a long time for your healing. Perhaps your situation has deteriorated, like Lazarus's body with each day in the tomb. Maybe the doctor keeps giving you negative reports and it seems hopeless in the natural. But let me tell you: God can still resurrect your situation! He raised Lazarus from the dead after four days and Jesus from the dead after three days. I'm pretty sure He can handle your situation. He has *all* power and nothing is impossible with Him. One touch from Him can turn everything around. Every day, shake yourself out of any discouragement or passive acceptance of your situation, stir your faith up, and declare, "Lord, even now, I still believe You can heal me!"

God promised Abraham and Sarah that they would give birth to an heir when they were 75 and 65 years old, respectively. In the natural, it was impossible since they were well beyond childbearing years. Adding to the impossibility, it took 25 years for the promise to be fulfilled, so they did not have Isaac until they were one hundred years old and ninety years old (Genesis 17:17). During this long waiting period, Abraham and Sarah had to dig their heels in and actively maintain their "I still believe" faith. The Bible says, "Even when there was no reason for hope, Abraham kept hoping . . . [because He was] fully convinced that God was able to do what he had promised" (Romans 4:18 NLT, 21 ESV).

God gave Joseph two powerful dreams about his future, and his brothers got jealous and sold him into slavery. He spent thirteen years in Egypt—first as a slave in Potiphar's house and then in prison—before those dreams came to pass. Joseph had to have some "I still believe" faith as he persevered through some horrible and unfair trials. But his faith paid off because he became the prime minister of Egypt, second in command to Pharaoh, and saved his whole family from famine.

After God sent the prophet Samuel to anoint David to be the next king of Israel, David had to wait fifteen years before finally taking the throne. During much of this intervening period, he was on the run from King Saul, who was trying to kill him, and living in caves. He had to have some serious "I still believe" faith. But it paid off because he became the greatest king in Israel's history and an ancestor of Jesus.

It was only supposed to be an eleven-day journey for the Israelites to go to the Promised Land. But because they complained, forgot how God supernaturally delivered them from Egypt, and were weak in faith, they wandered in the wilderness for forty years. But the Bible says Joshua and Caleb had a "different spirit" and never wavered in their faith (Numbers 14:24, 30). Because of their "I still believe" faith, they were the only two out of over two million Israelites who left Egypt to enter the Promised Land.

It's easy to be a doubter. It's easy to get discouraged and give up. People who do this are a dime a dozen. I'm asking you to be like Martha, Abraham, Joseph, David, and Joshua and Caleb and have a never-give-up, "I still believe" faith. Don't believe the "never" and "forever" lies. It doesn't matter how long you've been battling your illness; God can heal you with one touch. He's the God of suddenlies!

Father, help me to have a strong, never-give-up, "I still believe" faith. Help me to keep believing even when I don't see anything happening or when my situation has gotten worse. Thank You that You always come through in Your perfect timing. In Jesus' name I pray, Amen.

# Reflections and Prayers

What are your key takeaways from the past seven days?

_____

_____

_____

_____

_____

Based on those takeaways, what action steps could you implement to help your journey to healing?

_____

_____

_____

_____

_____

Use this space to write your current prayer requests to God and anything God has spoken to you about your situation through His Word, the Holy Spirit, people, dreams, or other means.

# DAY 29

# Help My Unbelief

Lord, I believe; help my unbelief!

Mark 9:24

I n *God Heals*, I covered extensively how faith is the most important and indispensable key to your healing (Mark 5:34; Matthew 9:28–30; Mark 10:52; Matthew 8:13; Mark 2:5; Luke 5:17–26; Acts 14:8–10). God cares about your needs, but He responds to your faith. Faith is the currency of heaven. Your healing is not just up to God. He has all power, but He needs you to have faith to receive it. What you believe will have a great impact on what happens.

The Bible says that after God did amazing miracles to deliver the Israelites from slavery in Egypt, including parting the Red Sea, the Israelites got a little way into the wilderness and began to grumble and doubt. Their unbelief limited what God wanted to do in their lives: "Yes, again and again they tempted God, and *limited the Holy One of Israel*. They did not remember His power" (Psalm 78:41–42). When Jesus went back to His hometown, He could not do any mighty works there because of their unbelief: "Now He could do no mighty work there, except that He laid His hands on a few sick people and healed them. And He marveled because of their unbelief" (Mark 6:5–6). Notice, it doesn't say He *would not* do mighty works. He had the desire to do them, but it says He *could not*. God only works by faith (James 1:6–7).

If we are honest, all of us have doubt and unbelief at times. Nobody has perfect faith. The good news is, God doesn't expect us to. He is not a perfectionist sitting up in heaven with His arms crossed, shaking His head in disapproval when we have doubts and fears. He knows our human frame, and He is full of mercy and grace (Psalm 103:13–14). This is clearly seen in the story of the man who brought his son to Jesus for healing (Mark 9:14–29).

From the time he was a young child, this son had violent seizures. A demonic spirit had thrown him into the fire and tried to drown him. I'm sure the father had taken the boy to doctors and tried everything he could to help him. Now he was seeking help from Jesus' disciples. By this time, they had helped heal and deliver many people. The disciples tried to cast the spirit out but were unable. So the father approached Jesus, pleading for Him to help his son.

Jesus told the man, "If you can believe, all things are possible to him who believes" (Mark 9:23). This is one of my favorite Bible verses, a blank-check promise about the power of faith. Notice how Jesus put it back on the man and said that all things would be possible if he had the faith for it. The man cried out with tears, "Lord, I believe; help my unbelief!" (Mark 9:24). What a vulnerable and honest response that I'm sure we can all relate to at times. I respect this man's honesty, and I believe Jesus did too. He didn't rebuke the man and say, "Too bad, you have unbelief. I'm not healing your son." No, He was full of compassion and grace. He honored what faith the man had and healed his son. When all you have is a mustard seed of faith, that's still enough for a miracle (Luke 17:6)!

One night, Jesus' disciples were in a boat on the Sea of Galilee when they saw Jesus walking on the water. At first, they were afraid it was a ghost, and Peter said, "Lord, if it is You, command me to come to You on the water" (Matthew 14:28). What audacious faith for Peter to believe he could walk on the water! But Jesus meant what He said: "If you can believe, all things are possible" (Mark 9:23). On Jesus' prompting, Peter stepped out of the boat and did what no mortal before him or since has ever done. He walked on water. But then the wind and waves kicked up, and Peter got afraid. He began to sink in the water. Jesus didn't say, "Too bad, Peter. You got afraid and doubted. I'm going to let you drown." No, like He did with the man with the epileptic son, Jesus had mercy on Peter. He *immediately* reached out His hand and lifted Peter up. God doesn't judge or abandon you when your faith gets wobbly. He reaches down in love and lifts you up.

---

Father, help me to stretch my faith and believe You for my healing, but thank You that You don't require perfect faith. You are full of grace and mercy and lift me up when my faith is weak. I praise You for being such a loving Abba, Daddy. In Jesus' name, Amen.

# DAY 30

# Be a Faith Warrior

> Fight the good fight of faith.
>
> 1 Timothy 6:12

As I have ministered to countless patients and their families over the years, I have noticed two kinds of people. One kind passively accepts what the doctor says as if it is gospel, and they don't have much faith for God to supernaturally heal them. Perhaps they started out with faith when they first got diagnosed, but their healing didn't come as quickly as they hoped, so their faith waned. The second kind of people are a rarer breed. They respect doctors but understand that God alone is their Healer and He has the final say. They believe God over all else. They have bulldog faith for their miracle, focus on God more than their sickness, and declare His Word over themselves relentlessly. They have a fighting spirit. They are faith warriors. These are the people who receive healing miracles. You get to decide which kind of person you will be. I'm asking you to be a faith warrior.

Hebrews 10:38 says, "Now the just shall live by faith; *but if anyone draws back, my soul has no pleasure in him*." God's love for us never changes, but make no mistake: He blesses and honors faith warriors. He said His "soul has no pleasure" when we "draw back" in adversity. The Israelites complained in the wilderness and were negative and weak in their faith. Because of this, they never entered the Promised Land. The only two people from that generation allowed in were Joshua and Caleb, who said, "Let us go up at once and take possession, for we are well able" (Numbers 13:30). They were faith warriors. Joshua was such a fighter that he asked God to make the sun stand still so they could keep fighting. And God did! It's the only time in history the sun stood still. God responds mightily to audacious faith.

David was another faith warrior. He took on the giant Goliath with a slingshot when the whole army of Israel was paralyzed with fear. He told Goliath, "You come against me with sword and spear and javelin, but I come against you in the name of the LORD Almighty. . . . This day the LORD will deliver you into my hands" (1 Samuel 17:45–46 NIV). God loved David's moxie and courageous faith and called him a man after His own heart (1 Samuel 13:14). The apostle Paul was beaten, stoned, shipwrecked three times, thrown into prison several times, and made to suffer many other things, but he just kept going. In one passage, the Jews stoned Paul, dragged him out of the city, and left him for dead. Instead of seeking refuge in another city, Paul got up and went right back into the city where he'd been stoned (Acts 14:19–20). No adversity could stop him. He wrote to his young protégé, Timothy, urging him to "fight the good fight of faith" (1 Timothy 6:12). Later, he wrote again, "I have fought the good fight . . . I have kept the faith" (2 Timothy 4:7). I pray that is your testimony, as well. Keep fighting the good fight of faith! Never give up! God is about to do astonishing things in your life!

When the Shunammite woman's son died, she told her husband, "It is well," put her son's body on Elisha's bed, and journeyed to see the prophet Elisha. When questioned by Elisha's servant, she repeated, "It is well." She stared death in the face with unflinching faith and didn't blink. Because of her steely faith, her son was raised from the dead.

The persistent widow kept knocking on the unjust judge's door at night while he was sleeping and refused to go away until she got justice. And she did.

The woman with the issue of blood refused to give up after suffering twelve years and spending all her money on doctors, only to get worse. Despite being banned from contact with anyone because of her condition, she pushed her way through the crowd to get to Jesus. She was the only one in that crowd who received a miracle. Everybody else had needs, but she brought her dogged persistence and radical faith.

God put stories like this in the Bible over and over to teach us the importance of being a faith warrior. We serve a faith God. He only works by faith. The Scripture says we can't expect to receive anything from God without faith and that it is impossible to please Him without faith (James 1:6–7; Hebrews 11:6). To be sure, God has grace and mercy on us when we are weak, as discussed in Day 29: "Help My Unbelief," but He wants us to mature and become faith warriors.

Heavenly Father, help me to be a faith warrior who believes You above all else and never gives up until my healing manifests. In Jesus' mighty name, Amen.

# DAY 31

# When, God, When?

How long, O LORD?

Psalm 13:1

I n Psalm 13:1, David wrote, "How long, O LORD? Will You forget me forever? How long will You hide Your face from me?" He was in the middle of a difficult waiting period. The prophet Samuel had already anointed him to be the next king of Israel, but before that promise was fulfilled, David spent years living in caves, running from King Saul, who was trying to kill him. All of us have felt like David at times when we're going through a trial and our flesh is weary and our emotions tattered. Over the many years I have ministered to the sick, I have seen numerous people instantly healed of blindness, deafness, paralysis, severe pain, and other medical conditions. I've lost count of how many tumors I've seen vanish. God moved suddenly in these situations, but there was a waiting period before the miracle, when the person had to stand in faith and fight through some challenges.

When God makes us wait, He's not being mean or uncaring. He always has the best plan for us. There is a preparation season before we receive what God has for us. Hebrews 6:12 says, "Imitate those who through faith and patience inherit the promises." We need both—faith and patience—to inherit the promises of God. He's not just concerned about healing us as quickly as possible; He's trying to do a work in us first. He wants our roots to go deeper in Him. He wants to build our character, toughen us to adversity, develop our spiritual muscles, and so much more. Nothing accomplishes these objectives better than going through times of adversity.

God's delays are not His denials. His timing is perfect. Our times are in His hands (Psalm 31:15). The Scripture says, "There is an appointed time for everything . . . under heaven . . . a time to heal" (Ecclesiastes 3:1, 3 NASB). There is a set time for your healing, a *kairos* moment.[1] Though it may tarry, it will not be late one second (Habakkuk 2:3).

You don't have to live upset and frustrated because your healing is not happening on your timetable. Psalm 37:7 says, "Rest in the LORD, and wait patiently for Him." You can rest, knowing that God loves you with a perfect love, He has the best plan for your life, and He is going to heal you in His perfect timing. When you are at rest, you are in faith. When you're frustrated and upset, you're not in faith. Release the frustration. Release the need to know why, when, or how. Waiting doesn't have to be miserable when we truly trust God and His timing.

My friend Christopher was diagnosed with lupus at the age of seventeen. It was an aggressive form that attacked his heart and other vital organs. Eventually, he needed a heart and kidney transplant. Christopher spent a year and a half in and out of the hospital receiving treatments and waiting for his new organs to become available. He had to have an LVAD pump installed to help pump his heart. During this time, I never heard Christopher complain. When he felt down or discouraged, he would read his Bible, put on some praise music, or listen to an inspiring sermon to encourage his faith. He kept Scriptures taped up all over his house and hospital room and declared the Word of God over himself daily. He continued to volunteer at the church whenever he was physically able, often with great difficulty. The day finally came when God moved suddenly, and he got a perfect match for his heart and two kidneys at the same time. The timing was nothing short of a miracle. Today, Christopher is healthy and vibrant and living his best life.

*How you act while you are waiting will have a big influence on the outcome.* It was only supposed to take eleven days for the Israelites to get to the Promised Land, but while they were in the wilderness, they murmured and complained, doubted God, were unthankful, and forgot the mighty works

He had done for them.[2] So they wandered in the wilderness for forty years and never made it into the Promised Land. Don't be like the Israelites. Be like my friend Christopher. Stay in faith. Stay thankful. Keep declaring the victory. God has a Promised Land waiting for you!

Father God, while I am waiting for my healing to manifest, help me to keep the right attitude, stay in faith, and trust You and Your perfect timing. In Jesus' name, Amen.

# DAY 32

## Praise Your Way to Victory

Heal me, LORD, and I will be healed . . . for you are the one I praise.

Jeremiah 17:14 NIV

There are few things that will position you to receive a miracle more than regularly praising God. The Scripture says God *inhabits* the praises of His people (Psalm 22:3 KJV). When our praises go up, His presence comes down and invades our situation. Praise attracts God's presence and miracle-working power like a magnet. It is an often-underutilized superpower that can shift the spiritual atmosphere around you and spark breakthrough. When you praise God, you give Him an all-access VIP pass to come in and move mightily in your situation. Are you ready for your victory? Then start praising!

I have a nonprofit organization called Living Hope Chaplaincy that trains volunteers to provide spiritual care to hospital patients and their families. We have teams of volunteers in many hospitals who have ministered to tens of thousands of patients. Our volunteers often sing hymns or praise songs with patients and spend time worshiping the Lord with them. Frequently, there is a palpable shift in the atmosphere as the weight and glory of God's presence enters the room. Fear and heaviness melt like wax in His presence. Often, the patient cries as the Holy Spirit ministers to them. We have seen more miracles happen in this environment of praise than at any other time.

Whereas gratitude is thanking God for what He has done, praise is exalting Him for *who He is*. He is good all the time and worthy of our praise, regardless of our circumstances. He is God Almighty, who has all power and authority. He knows all things and sees all things. He is present everywhere, all the time, both in us and around us, closer than the air we breathe. He is our Savior, Healer, Deliverer, Helper, Strengthener, Comforter, Counselor, Protector, Provider, and much more. He is everything we need Him to be. He is perfect, holy, merciful, gracious, faithful, and mighty. David said, "I will praise the LORD at all times. I will constantly speak his praises" (Psalm 34:1 NLT). I'm asking you to open your mouth and give God praise every day, no matter how you are feeling or what your situation looks like. It is a key to your healing and victory!

When King Jehoshaphat was surrounded by three enemy armies with no way out in the natural, he prayed to God, "We have no power against this great multitude . . . nor do we know what to do, but our eyes are upon You" (2 Chronicles 20:12). God instructed him to send the praise team out in front of the army, and when he did, God sent confusion upon the three enemy armies, and they destroyed each other. This is why the Scripture says God is "fearful in praises" (Exodus 15:11). Like Jehoshaphat, it may look like you are surrounded by sickness, bad reports, even financial and other woes. But God is surrounding what is surrounding you. He is fighting your battles in the unseen realm. He can make a way where there seems to be no way. Keep praising Him, and you will see the victory!

The praises of Joshua and the Israelites brought down the walls of Jericho. When David praised with his harp, King Saul was delivered from a tormenting spirit. When the enemy is tormenting you with fear, discouragement, even insomnia, praise is the best relief. Paul and Silas's praises at midnight in a Roman prison caused God to send an earthquake that opened the prison doors and loosed the chains of every prisoner. It was a praise-quake! Praise will free you from every chain. Over and over in the Bible, we see that praise brings miracles and victory.

*Well, Pastor Steve, this sounds nice, but I don't feel like praising God. I don't really have much to praise Him about.*

*My situation isn't good.* Praise is not just something we do in church when everything is wonderful in our lives. Anybody can praise God then. You have to rule over your flesh and feelings and praise Him when You don't feel like it. Put on some praise and worship music. Let it shift the atmosphere and redirect your mind off your problems and onto God. Praising God in the tough times is one of the best expressions of faith. It moves the heart of God. He can't resist a praiser! All through the day, say, "Father, I praise You because You are good all the time. You are my Healer and Deliverer. Nothing is impossible with You! I give You praise, glory, and honor for my healing that's on the way." When you do this, you are paving the way for your miracle!

---

Heavenly Father, help my mouth to be filled with Your praises. In Jesus' name, Amen.

# DAY 33

# Your Helper

And I will pray the Father, and He will give you another Helper, that He may abide with you forever . . . for He dwells with you and will be in you.

John 14:16–17

A serious health challenge is one of the toughest trials anyone can experience—whether it's your own or a close family member's. I know this from my own health challenges, as well as those of my family members and the thousands of sick people I've ministered to for 25 years. Fortunately, God gave us a supernatural Helper to help us victoriously navigate every challenge we face in life: His Holy Spirit, who lives inside every believer. Today, I want to highlight some specific ways the Holy Spirit can help you navigate your health challenge victoriously:

1. **Comforter.** The Bible calls God the "God of all comfort" (2 Corinthians 1:3; see also Romans 15:5). His Holy Spirit is called the "Comforter" four times (John 14:16, 26; 15:26; 16:7 KJV). In Psalm 23:4, David wrote, "Even when I walk through the darkest valley, I will not be afraid, for you are close beside me. Your rod and your staff protect and comfort me" (NLT). The Holy Spirit will wash over you with divine comfort and peace when you feel afraid, discouraged, or lonely.

2. **Counselor.** There are many important health-care and other decisions that have to be made on your journey to healing—which doctor to use, what treatment to pursue—or whether to undergo a certain medical treatment at all; whether hospitalization is necessary, and if so, what hospital to use; what to eat and not eat to help your healing process; and many more. The Holy Spirit is there to counsel and guide you so you make the best decisions according to God's will. Isaiah 11:2 calls Him the Spirit of wisdom and counsel. Psalm 32:8 says, "I will instruct you and teach you in the way you should go; I will counsel you with my loving eye on you" (NIV). Quiet your spirit and pay attention to the gentle promptings and "still small voice" of the Holy Spirit inside of you (1 Kings 19:12). He will never steer you wrong.

My friend Melinda shared how she felt a lump in her breast and went to her gynecologist for a mammogram. He was out on an extended vacation and the covering physician said, "He may or may not choose to remove the lump when he returns." She couldn't get a follow-up appointment for several weeks. As she was leaving the office, the Holy Spirit spoke to her in her spirit and said, "Turn around and go back and get the film from your mammogram and take it to an oncologist right away." She obeyed that prompting. It turned out she had a very aggressive form of breast cancer. She said had she not listened to the Holy Spirit, she would be dead today.

The Holy Spirit will also reveal if there is anything inside your heart, such as unforgiveness, that may be blocking your healing.[1] Daniel 2:22 (NIV) says, "He reveals deep and hidden things." Like David did in Psalm 139:23–24, ask God to search you and reveal if there is anything blocking your breakthrough.

3. **Intercessor.** Romans 8:26 says, "The Spirit helps us in our weakness. For we do not know what to pray for as we ought, but the Spirit himself intercedes for us with groanings too deep for words" (ESV). When you don't know how or what to pray, or when you feel too weak or tired to pray, the Holy Spirit has you covered and intercedes with the Father on your behalf.

4. **Strengthener.** The Holy Spirit is called our Strengthener (John 14:16 AMP). You may feel weak sometimes, but the Holy Spirit inside of you is greater and stronger

than anything you face. He will strengthen you to persevere and stay in faith when you feel like giving up. When you are going in for a test, treatment, or procedure, the Holy Spirit will give you supernatural strength and help you to be brave.

5. **Standby.** David wrote, "Where can I go from Your Spirit? Or where can I flee from Your presence?" (Psalm 139:7). You may feel alone at times, but the Holy Spirit is always *in* you and *with* you. He is available 24 hours a day, seven days a week. He never sleeps, never gets distracted, and is never too busy for you. You will never call on Him and get a busy signal or voice mail. He is always there to assist you any way you need it.

---

Father, thank You for the countless ways Your Holy Spirit has already helped me and will continue to help me navigate this health challenge victoriously. In Jesus' name, Amen.

# DAY 34

# Heavenly Helpers

He shall give His angels charge over you.

Psalm 91:11

God has given you everything you need to win the battle for your health and live a victorious life. One of those things is an army of powerful angels to help you in life and in your healing journey. God created these mighty spiritual beings to serve Him and His people. They are His messengers, they execute His Word, and they encourage, care for, and protect believers. Angels are referred to around three hundred times in the Bible. You may never see an angel (although many have), but the unseen spirit realm is more real than what you see with your natural eyes.

You are surrounded by angels, who are there to help you in many ways. You are not in this fight alone.

The prophet Elijah went through a period when he felt exhausted and depressed, and he wanted to die. An angel came and ministered to him twice and was instrumental in his recovery (1 Kings 19:1–8). After Jesus spent forty days in the wilderness being tempted by the devil, He felt depleted and weak in His humanity. Matthew 4:11 says, "Then the devil left Him, and behold, angels came and *ministered to Him*." Another time, Jesus was in the Garden of Gethsemane, grieving about His impending death so intensely that He was sweating drops of blood. Luke 22:43 says, "Then an angel appeared to Him from heaven, *strengthening Him*."

Angels were not just for people like Elijah and Jesus in the Bible; they are for you and me today. Hebrews 1:14 says angels are "*ministering spirits sent forth to minister* for those who will inherit salvation." God will send angels to minister to you and strengthen you when you feel down, discouraged, or weak. You will feel a sudden lifting of your heaviness, a shift in the atmosphere, and a strange peace and calm wash over you. An angel may even be disguised as a person who ministers to you or helps you somehow. Hebrews 13:2 says, "Do not forget to show hospitality to strangers, for by so doing some people have shown hospitality to angels without knowing it" (NIV). I have heard many stories from patients I have ministered to over the years about people who gave them special care or uncommon favor in the hospital, at a doctor's office, or somewhere else and then they never saw that person again. God has His people and His angels everywhere to help you!

Angels even help with healing. The Gospel of John says, "An angel went down at a certain time into the pool [of Bethesda] and stirred up the water; then whoever stepped in first, after the stirring of the water, *was made well of whatever disease he had*" (John 5:4). I read a powerful testimony about a woman who went through a recurrence of thyroid cancer and a deluge of other personal trials. As she lay on the MRI table, she felt grieved and overwhelmed. She began to pray, repeating Isaiah 53:4, about Jesus bearing our griefs and carrying our sorrows. She said, "As I finished praying those words, the atmosphere of the room changed. I can't explain it except to say I was in the presence of two angel-like beings. One stood tall on my left with arms folded across his chest, as if he was guarding me. The other stood very close on my right." An incredible feeling of peace and comfort enveloped her. It wasn't long after that she was totally healed.[1]

Angels also protect you everywhere you go, from danger, accidents, even human error from doctors or other medical personnel. The Scripture says, "[God] will order his angels to protect you wherever you go. They will hold you up with their hands" (Psalm 91:11–12 NLT). You can rest and be at peace, knowing that God's angels have your back.

Finally, angels do battle for you in the spirit realm against the forces of darkness. Psalm 34:7 says, "The angel of the

LORD encamps all around those who fear Him, and delivers them." When Daniel prayed, God dispatched an angel with the answer to his prayer, but a demonic spirit intercepted that angel and battled with him to stop the answer to Daniel's prayer. Backup was sent to help that angel, and Daniel's answer came after 21 days (Daniel 10:12–13). This is one reason we need to be persistent in prayer. Sometimes there is demonic interference in the unseen realm, and we must show the enemy we are more determined than he is.

Father, thank You for Your mighty angels that have been given charge over me and help me on my healing journey. In Jesus' name, Amen.

# DAY 35

# Your Authority in Christ

Behold, I give you the authority to trample on serpents and
scorpions, and over all the power of the enemy.

Luke 10:19

In life, we understand that police must use their authority
to keep society orderly and safe. Parents use their authority
to train their young children and keep them safe. Teach-
ers use their authority with their students. Today, I want to
talk to you about the spiritual authority you have in Christ.
The apostle Paul wrote in Ephesians 6:12 (NLT) that "we are
not fighting against flesh-and-blood enemies, but . . . against
evil spirits in the heavenly places" (NLT). "Heavenly places"
refers to the spiritual atmosphere around us where these
evil spirits and God's angels operate. These spirits attack

people's health, minds, finances, relationships, and anything else they can. Paul tells us three times in this passage that we have to "stand" against these spirits, which means to *actively resist* and *fight against* them (Ephesians 6:10–13, 14). The good news is that Jesus has given us spiritual authority to kick these demonic spirits out of our lives. But this authority does us no good if we don't use it. If you are going to reclaim your health and live a victorious life, you must actively and regularly use your authority in Christ.

Jesus said in Luke 10:19, "Behold, *I give you the authority* to trample on serpents and scorpions, and over all the power of the enemy." "Serpents and scorpions" in this verse symbolizes demonic spirits. Jesus said we are to trample on them. *Trample* is not a passive, genteel word. In this context, it is a battle term that means to stomp on and crush. When you are battling a serious illness, perhaps even fighting for your life, it's not time for passivity or patty-cakes. This is war!

When I was in my early thirties, before I knew anything about spiritual warfare, I used to get panic attacks. I would wake up in the middle of the night sweating, my heart racing, feeling like I was going to die. These attacks came on me suddenly for no apparent reason. I began taking anxiety medication, but it didn't help much. Then I started learning about spiritual warfare and the spiritual authority Jesus has given every believer. One day, the Lord spoke to me—not out loud, but down in my spirit—and said, *Those panic attacks are from a spirit. You have to take authority over it.* The next time I had an attack, I said out loud in a firm voice, "I command every spirit of panic, fear, stress, and torment to go from me in the name of Jesus and never come back." Almost immediately, the attack stopped. I repeated this strategy a few more times when the panic attacks returned, and each time it worked, until finally I was totally free. I haven't had another panic attack in over 25 years. God used that experience to open my eyes to the reality of spiritual warfare and how powerful our authority in Christ is.

In the Gospels, we see that these demonic forces can cause sickness in people's bodies and Jesus often had to confront them to heal someone. The Scripture says that Jesus "went about doing good and *healing all who were oppressed by the devil*" (Acts 10:38). In other words, many people received their healing when Jesus delivered them from demonic oppression. For example, He healed a woman who'd had a medical condition for eighteen years that caused her to be bent over. The Scripture says her condition was caused by a "*spirit of infirmity*" (Luke 13:11). Jesus said she was bound by Satan, and when He dealt with this spirit of infirmity, the woman was healed (Luke 13:16). In another passage, a young boy's seizures were caused by a demonic spirit. When Jesus took authority over the spirit, the boy was healed. *Fully one-third of Jesus' healings involved spiritual warfare.*

I am not suggesting that you have a demon because you are sick or that all sickness is caused by demonic spirits, just that they can and do attack people's bodies. Even when they are not the cause, they are always looking for a vulnerability and will try to attack you with fear, vexing thoughts, and other ways. The enemy will fight you for your healing. Ignoring these spirits or pretending they don't exist is not a winning strategy. In tomorrow's devotional, I will cover how to use your authority in Christ effectively to take back your health, peace, joy, and victory.

***

Jesus, thank You for giving me spiritual authority over all the power of the enemy. Help me to use my authority to reclaim my health and walk in victory. In Jesus' name, Amen.

# Reflections and Prayers

What are your key takeaways from the past seven days?

_____

_____

_____

_____

Based on those takeaways, what action steps could you implement to help your journey to healing?

_____

_____

_____

_____

_____

Use this space to write your current prayer requests to God and anything God has spoken to you about your situation through His Word, the Holy Spirit, people, dreams, or other means.

# DAY 36

# How to Use
# Your Authority in Christ

[Jesus] cast out the spirits with a word, and healed all who
were sick.

Matthew 8:16

Yesterday, I talked about the spiritual warfare involved
in your healing journey. Every person is involved in
spiritual warfare, whether they realize it or not. First
Peter 5:8–9 says, "Be sober, be vigilant; because *your adversary the devil* walks about like a roaring lion, seeking whom
he may devour. *Resist him*, steadfast in the faith, knowing
that *the same sufferings are experienced by your brotherhood
in the world*." This passage is packed with information. First,
it tells us who our adversary is. It's not other people. It's

not God. It is the devil. Second, it says we must *resist him*. One of the main ways we do this is by using our spiritual authority in Christ. Third, it says the enemy causes "sufferings" that are common around the world. Jesus said, "The thief comes only to steal and kill and destroy" (John 10:10 ESV). The enemy will steal and destroy your health, peace, joy, and other things if you allow him to. If you're going to win the battle for your health and walk in victory, you must use the authority Jesus has given you. Today, I want to cover how to do this effectively.

We use our authority over the enemy by opening our mouth and commanding him to go in Jesus' name. Jesus and His disciples never prayed away demonic spirits. They used their authority and cast them out or commanded them to go. Matthew 8:16 says Jesus "cast out the spirits *with a word* and healed all who were sick." In Mark 1:25, "Jesus rebuked [an evil spirit], saying, 'Be quiet, and come out of him!'" The word *rebuke* here means to talk sternly to. When addressing the enemy, speak firmly and authoritatively. One time, a girl with a spirit of divination kept harassing Paul, Silas, and Timothy as they were ministering in Philippi. Finally, "Paul . . . said to the spirit, 'I command you in the name of Jesus Christ to come out of her.' And he came out that very hour" (Acts 16:18). Notice in these examples that Jesus and Paul *spoke directly to the spirits out loud and commanded them to go*. Anytime you address a demonic spirit, always say "in the name of Jesus," because that is where your authority comes from.

During the many years I have ministered to thousands of sick people, these are some of the most common demonic spirits people encounter on their healing journey: spirits of infirmity (sickness), fear, depression, oppression, discouragement, despair, hopelessness, anxiety, and worry, as well as tormenting spirits, lying spirits, and spirits of insomnia. We need not be afraid or intimidated by these spirits because we have authority over them in Jesus' name. In Luke 10:17, the seventy disciples Jesus sent out returned and said, "Lord, even the demons are subject to us in Your name."

After we have commanded them to go in Jesus' name, the next step is to declare out loud what the Word of God says. When the devil tempted Jesus three times in the wilderness, each time Jesus responded by saying, "It is written . . . ," quoting a Scripture that countered what the devil said (Matthew 4:4, 7, 10). Finally, He said, "Away with you, Satan!" (Matthew 4:10). His mouth was the tool by which He used his authority.

Using Jesus and His disciples as our examples, suppose you are struggling with fear. Fear is a natural human emotion, but there is also a spirit of fear that stalks us at times. When you feel that intense spirit of fear, say, "In the name of Jesus, I command the spirit of fear to go from me and never come back. According to 2 Timothy 1:7, I declare that God has not given me a spirit of fear, but of power, love, and a sound mind. I reject fear and receive God's love and peace, in Jesus' name." This approach works for depression, insomnia, or any other spirit that attacks you.

It's not just demonic spirits over which we have authority. When Peter's mother was sick, Jesus healed her by rebuking her fever. Luke 4:39 says, "He stood over her and rebuked the fever, and it left her." Remember, Jesus said believers can do the same works He did because His Holy Spirit lives inside them (John 14:12). He also said in Mark 11:23 that we can tell a mountain to be removed and be cast into the sea. When we can tell a mountain what to do, that's authority. Your "mountain" is your sickness. You can speak directly to your sickness and symptoms and command them to leave your body, in Jesus' name.

Jesus, help me to use the authority You've given me regularly and effectively. In Your precious name, I pray, Amen.

# DAY 37

## Healthy Soul

Beloved, I pray that you may prosper in all things and be in health, *just as your soul prospers.*

3 John 2

E veryone has been hurt by other people and life at some point and has pockets of pain in their soul. God not only wants to heal your body; He wants to heal your soul. His vision is for your entire being to be healthy and thriving so you can become all He created you to be and fulfill every plan and purpose He has for your life. Third John 2 says, "Beloved, I pray that you may prosper in all things and be in health, *just as your soul prospers.*" Notice, we will prosper and be in good health *as our soul prospers.* The health of our soul affects every area of our lives—every decision we make, our relationships, finances, career, and physical health. Statistics show that up to 90 percent of illnesses are caused by negative thoughts and emotions.[1] In fact, the word *disease* is a compound of the root words *dis* and *ease*, which mean "against ease." Lack of peace in our soul makes us vulnerable to disease. Good health and victory start on the inside.

Our souls are comprised of our mind, will, and emotions. It is where we harbor all the pain caused by other people—as well as the bad memories, betrayals, rejection, mistakes, failures, and negative thoughts and emotions we experience. Most of our problems are caused by our souls, not our born-again, sanctified spirits. It's unhealthiness and pain in our souls that cause us to make bad choices in our lives, abuse drugs and alcohol, not take care of our bodies, have unhealthy relationships, and many other bad things that happen in our lives. After salvation, our top priority should be healing and freedom in our souls.

Kintsugi is a fascinating Japanese art form that dates to the fifteenth century. Broken pieces of pottery are glued back together, and the fault lines are then gilded over with lines of gold. The word *kintsugi* means "to join with gold." It symbolizes our broken places being healed and turned into a thing of beauty. Rather than discarding or trying to hide the broken pieces, in kintsugi they are highlighted with gold and made the most important part. The resulting piece is more beautiful and valuable than it was before it was broken.

That's what God does with us when we allow Him to heal the broken, hurt places in our soul. The prophet Jeremiah had a vision of God as the Potter and us as the clay. He said, "The vessel that he made of *clay was marred* in the hand of the potter; so *he made it again into another vessel, as it seemed good to the potter* to make" (Jeremiah 18:4). God wants to take the marred places in your soul, heal and restore you, and remake you into a better version of yourself.

David said, "He restores my soul" (Psalm 23:3). Here are two important keys to allow God to heal and restore your soul:

1. **Let it go.** When you don't let go of things, they never heal. There was a trap devised for monkeys where a banana was placed in a barrel that had a small hole in it. When a monkey reached his arm into the hole and grabbed the banana, he could not get his hand back out. The only way to get free was to let go of the banana. Often, that's how we are with our hurts. God is trying to heal us and set us free, but we won't let go of them. God is not going to forcefully remove them from us. We must choose to release past hurts, unforgiveness, mistakes, failures, and disappointments. Holding on will keep us stuck where we are and hinder our physical healing.

2. **Invite God into all the hurt places in your soul.** We can't expect God to heal what we don't give Him access to.

We have to get honest with ourselves, deal with our soul hurts and toxins, and ask God to heal and restore our souls. Jesus said, "Behold, I stand at the door and knock. If anyone hears My voice and opens the door, I will come in to him" (Revelation 3:20). Jesus is knocking at the door of your soul. Let Him come in and give you total healing and freedom in your soul.

Heavenly Father, I choose to let go of everything in my soul that is not of You. I ask You to come in and heal my soul so I can become all You created me to be. In Jesus' name, Amen.

# DAY 38

## Forgiveness

If you do not forgive men their trespasses, neither will your Father forgive your trespasses.

Matthew 6:15

Margaret Green had a traumatic upbringing with a father who physically and verbally abused her daily. One of her father's friends then molested her for three years. At the age of eight, she attempted suicide. As a teen, she became promiscuous, using and selling drugs. At 21, she had four children and stripped and sold drugs to provide for them. One night after a party, she was violently raped and left for dead. After that, she gave up her life to Christ, gave up her old lifestyle, and eventually married a godly man. At 34 years old, she was diagnosed with two life-threatening conditions. Doctors only gave her a 5 percent chance of survival.

By this point in her life, Margaret and her husband had been fervent believers in Christ for years. They prayed in faith every day for Margaret's condition, relentlessly declared the Word of God over her, and did everything they knew to do, but nothing changed for two years. One day, the Lord spoke to Margaret in her spirit and said, *I need you to forgive everyone who has ever hurt you*. When she did that with His help, she was miraculously healed. Doctors were baffled and said there was no medical explanation for her healing.[1]

That is the power of forgiveness. Often, it is the linchpin to a person receiving their healing or breakthrough. So often, we think we're waiting on God, but God is waiting on us to do what He's told us to do. Many times, I have seen people receive their healing quickly after choosing to forgive someone who hurt them.

In Mark 11:25, Jesus said, "Whenever you stand praying, if you have anything against anyone, forgive him, that your Father in heaven may also forgive you your trespasses." He was saying, "Don't even bother praying if you have unforgiveness in your heart." *If you are harboring unforgiveness, your prayers won't work*. Jesus also said, "If you do not forgive men their trespasses, neither will your Father forgive your trespasses" (Matthew 6:15). God will only forgive us when we forgive others. Remember this line from the Lord's

Prayer: "Forgive us our debts, *as* we forgive our debtors" (Matthew 6:12)? When we refuse to forgive, God will not forgive us our trespasses. That means we are not in right standing with Him and He can't bless us the way He wants to. *Unforgiveness is one of the biggest blocks to receiving healing and God's blessings.*

All of us have been hurt by other people, including those closest to us. People are flawed, and we say and do things that hurt each other from time to time. Our sense of justice expects the person who hurt us to pay us back or at least suffer consequences. But that is not how God treated us. There was no way to pay God back for our own sins, so He sent Jesus to pay the price for us on the cross. Because of Jesus' shed blood, God released us from our sins and the eternal punishment we deserved. How can we receive so much grace and forgiveness from God and then refuse to give it to others? Forgiveness means *release*. When we forgive those who hurt us, we release them and our pain to God. We release them from paying us back for what they did to us. The reality is, they can't pay us back. Only God can. And He will only pay us back if we forgive.

Choosing to forgive others not only releases them, *it releases us*. Our unforgiveness doesn't affect the other person one iota; it just makes us miserable and prevents us from living a victorious life. It's so not worth forfeiting your healing and all that God wants to do in your life by hanging on to unforgiveness. I understand that forgiveness can be difficult, but God never asks us to do something that He doesn't give us the ability to do. Ask God to help you forgive and He will.

———

Father, I choose right now to forgive everyone who has ever hurt me. I release them and my pain to You. I choose to forgive myself for all my mistakes and failures. Thank You that You have already forgiven me and have chosen not to remember my sins and mistakes (Isaiah 43:25; Psalm 103:12; Ephesians 4:32). Father, I forgive You if I have ever had anger toward You. Help me to truly forgive, and heal my soul so I can become all You created me to be. In Jesus' name, Amen.

# DAY 39

## Serve Somebody

Those who live to bless others will have blessings heaped upon them.

Proverbs 11:25 TPT

I t's easy when you are battling a serious illness to let it dominate your life. I have seen scores of people get swallowed up by their medical condition, and it becomes all they think about, talk about, post about, and pray about. But one of the secrets to healing your body and soul is to get outside of yourself and serve somebody else. Many people have told me over the years that serving others was critical to their healing. Isaiah 58:7–8 says, "Share your food with everyone who is hungry; share your home with the poor and homeless. Give clothes to those in need; don't turn away your relatives. *Then . . . you will quickly be healed*" (CEV). When you bless others, God promises you will quickly be healed.

Being absorbed in our own problems and needs does not bring us joy, nor does it cause God to bless us. What does is when we say, *God, this is hard and I need a breakthrough, but while I am waiting on You, show me somebody to whom I can be a blessing.* When you bless someone else, you are sowing a seed for your own need. The Scripture says, "Do not be deceived, God is not mocked; for whatever a man sows, that he will also reap" (Galatians 6:7).

My friend Sue, who was healed of two types of cancer, shares in her own words how serving others was critical in her healing process:

> As a massage therapist for humans, horses and canines, serving during my healing from two primary cancers had a profound impact on both my emotional well-being and physical healing. No matter how bad things were, it brought me great joy to make people and animals feel their best. It gave me a sense of purpose and meaning and allowed me to channel my energy into something positive and uplifting. Cancer can make you feel helpless and out of control, but serving others helped me regain a sense of control over my life. It reminded me that I still had the ability to make a positive impact even though I had physical challenges. Serving others also helped me gain perspective about my own situation. When you witness the struggles and hardships of others, it

puts your own challenges into perspective. It caused me to appreciate the things I still had and gave me an attitude of gratitude. Lastly, serving others gave me a social outlet and allowed me to build new friendships and develop a support network, which were healing for my soul.

The Scripture says, "Faith without works is dead" (James 2:20, 26). Our faith can't just be words and thoughts; it must have action behind it. Serving others is a way to put works to our faith. Even if you are bedridden in the hospital, you can encourage and pray for the health-care workers who come into your room. You can have dinner delivered to the family in the room next door. You can pray for others who need healing. Job 42:10 says that God healed Job and restored double everything he lost "*when he prayed for his friends.*" That is an incredible verse—Job was healed and restored when he prayed for others. Serving others could be the key to your miracle.

I shared in my first book, *God Heals*, how Dodie Osteen, the matriarch of Lakewood Church, was miraculously healed of stage 4 metastatic liver cancer in 1981 after doctors gave her only a few weeks to live. She got down to 89 pounds, was as yellow as a banana from jaundice, and could barely get out of bed, but she made herself go down to the church and pray for others. Today, she is a healthy, vibrant ninety-year-old who still does full-time ministry. She credits serving others as one of the keys to receiving her healing.

Jesus said, "Whoever wants to be great must become a servant. . . . That is what the Son of Man has done: He came to serve, not be served" (Matthew 20:26–28 MSG). Jesus washed His disciples' dirty feet and then said, "I have given you an example, that you should do as I have done to you" (John 13:15). The third time He appeared to His disciples after being resurrected, He cooked them breakfast while they were out fishing (John 21:1–14). He was always serving others and gave His life for us all in the ultimate act of service. As you follow His example and find ways to bless others, I am confident your own breakthrough will come.

—— — ——

Father, help me to get outside my own problems and needs and show me ways I can be a blessing to others. In Jesus' name, Amen.

# DAY 40

# Body Wise

Glorify God in your body.

1 Corinthians 6:20

have covered many spiritual principles in this devotional,
but today I want to get very practical. Jesus didn't just
preach to the five thousand; He took care of their practical need for food. I am a big believer in doing everything we
can in the natural to heal and having faith for God to do the
supernatural. When we do our part, God will do His part.
Our part includes being a good steward of the body God
has given us. Our body has an amazing ability to heal itself
when we give it the most nutritious food, exercise regularly,
and make other healthy lifestyle choices. I have seen countless
people defeat virtually every disease by doing everything they

can to take care of their bodies and by using the spiritual tools I discuss in this book and *God Heals*.

I am not a doctor or health expert, but a health enthusiast who has passionately studied health and wellness for over ten years. I have a group called *Healthy You* on Facebook that has over five thousand members from all over the world where I give daily health information. I am going to share with you some of the wisdom I have gleaned from the top natural medical doctors in the world. Nothing I say is meant for medical purposes, but educational purposes only. Please check with your health-care provider if you have any questions.

A jaw-dropping 88 percent of Americans are metabolically unhealthy because of their diet.[1] This is the root cause of virtually every disease. Studies show that 60 percent of the American diet is ultra-processed food.[2] These are packaged foods that have been substantially changed from their original state and contain additives, preservatives, and other chemicals. These foods are driving the explosion of cancer and chronic diseases in our society.

Below are some key ways you can help your body heal:

1. **Eat clean, living foods that God created.** Eat lots of organic produce; clean meats like grass-fed beef, natural chicken, and organic turkey; wild-caught (not farm-raised) fish; nuts and seeds. When you grocery-shop, stay on the perimeter of the store, where living foods

are found. The middle aisles have the ultra-processed, packaged foods.

2. **Avoid sugar and bad carbs like the plague.** "Bad carbs" are carbohydrates that spike your blood sugar, like potatoes, rice, corn and corn products (chips, tortillas, popcorn, etc.), and wheat and wheat products (breads, wheat flour, pasta, pizza crust, tortillas, cereals, etc.). Numerous studies point to sugar and bad carbs as the number-one enemy of good health. They wreak havoc on the body and make us vulnerable to disease by causing inflammation and insulin resistance (which most Americans have and don't realize it), depressing the immune system, damaging the gut, and other ways. Cancer cells thrive on sugar, as well.

3. **Avoid seed oils.** These ultra-processed oils dominate the oil aisle in the grocery store—canola, corn, "vegetable" oil, cottonseed, soybean, sunflower, safflower, grapeseed, and rice bran oil. They are also found in many food products. They are highly inflammatory and destructive to our health. Instead of these oils, cook with extra-virgin olive oil, grass-fed butter or ghee, avocado oil, or coconut oil.

4. **Strengthen your gut health.** Hippocrates, the father of Western medicine, said, "All disease begins in the gut." Our gut (or GI tract) is a complex ecosystem of over one hundred trillion bacteria and has a huge impact

on our health. Seventy percent of our immune system is in the gut. When our gut is unhealthy, it causes inflammation and makes us vulnerable to disease. Top gut destroyers are sugar and bad carbs, gluten (mainly wheat products), GMOs (mostly corn and soy products), stress, poor sleep, antibiotics, artificial sweeteners, painkillers like ibuprofen and acetaminophen, and processed foods. To improve your gut health, eat a lot of fiber and prebiotics (the food that good gut bacteria need to survive). Foods rich in prebiotics include garlic, onions, leeks, asparagus, dandelion leaves (use in salads and smoothies), jicama, cocoa, flax seeds, and seaweed salad. Also, take a high-quality probiotic supplement daily.

5. **Exercise.** If you are physically able, exercise helps to mitigate and reverse disease. It increases circulation and oxygenation in the body; burns off excess blood glucose and cortisol; helps with insulin resistance and weight loss; lowers blood pressure; releases feel-good, stress-fighting endorphins; and much more. Even if you are in the hospital, try to walk around or do whatever you can to move your body.

Heavenly Father, help me to be a great steward of my body and make wise dietary and other choices that will help my body heal. In Jesus' name, Amen.

# Reflections and Prayers

What are your key takeaways from the past five days?

_____

_____

_____

_____

_____

Based on those takeaways, what action steps could you implement to help your journey to healing?

_____

_____

_____

_____

_____

Use this space to write your current prayer requests to God and anything God has spoken to you about your situation through His Word, the Holy Spirit, people, dreams, or other means.

# Notes

### Day 3  All Inclusive

1. Bruce Hurt, "Salvation—Soteria: A Greek Word Study," Precept Austin, March 3, 2018, https://www.preceptaustin.org/salvation-soteria _greek_word_study; *Strong's Concordance* #4991.

### Day 4  Just Receive

1. The original Greek tense was continuous—"For she *kept saying* to herself . . ."

### Day 10  Whose Report Will You Believe?

1. "How Many People Were Raised from the Dead in the Bible?," The Bible Answer, October 27, 2017, https://thebibleanswer.org/how-many -raised-from-the-dead-bible.

### Day 11  This Is Only a Test

1. Other translations use the word *tempted* here, but the word *tested* is a better translation. The original Greek word is *peirazo*, which means "to be tested" (*Strong's Concordance* #3985).

## Day 13  A New Perspective

1. Steven Furtick, "Is Your Perspective Holding You Hostage?," video, Elevation Church Facebook Page, August 29, 2018, https://fb.watch /oK0BCe7rVF.

2. "How Many People Die Each Day in 2023?," World Population Review, accessed December 4, 2023, https://worldpopulationreview.com /countries/deaths-per-day.

3. "World Bank and WHO: Half the World Lacks Access to Essential Health Services, 100 Million Still Pushed into Extreme Poverty Because of Health Expenses," World Health Organization, December 13, 2017, https://www.who.int/news/item/13-12-2017-world-bank-and-who-half-the -world-lacks-access-to-essential-health-services-100-million-still-pushed -into-extreme-poverty-because-of-health-expenses.

4. Seyma Bayram, "Billions of People Lack Access to Clean Drinking Water, U.N. Report Finds," NPR, March 22, 2023, https://www.npr.org /2023/03/22/1165464857.

5. "Literacy," UNESCO Institute for Statistics, accessed December 4, 2023, https://uis.unesco.org/en/topic/literacy.

## Day 16  First See It on the Inside

1. Charles Duhigg, *The Power of Habit: Why We Do What We Do in Life and Business* (New York: Random House, 2023), 112.

2. "Healing the Incurable," *The 700 Club* YouTube channel, April 10, 2019, https://youtu.be/0eCFwVeoOBA.

## Day 19  It Is Well

1. Bethel Church Ripon, "Horatio Gates Spafford—The Story Behind the Hymn 'It Is Well With My Soul,'" December 12, 2018, www.bethelripon .com/life-stories/horatio-gates-spafford.

2. Corrie ten Boom, *Jesus Is Victor* (Tarrytown, NY: Fleming H. Revell, 1985), 183.

## Day 24  Whatever You Say

1. *The Lectionary Greek Bible Commentary* explains, "The woman was repeatedly saying to herself—not once—that if she touched him, she

would be healed" (*Lectionary Greek*, http://lectionarygreek.blogspot.com
/2009/06/mark-521-43.html?m=1). Mark 5:28 (AMPC) reads, "'For she *kept
saying*, If I only touch His garments, I shall be restored to health.'" *The
Passion Translation* reads: "For she *kept saying to herself*, 'If I could touch
even his clothes, I know I will be healed.'"

### Day 31  When, God, When?

1. *Strong's Concordance* #2540, *kairos*—"a set time or season."
2. Psalm 78 chronicles all the Israelites' waiting mistakes and is a study
in how *not* to wait.

### Day 33  Your Helper

1. See Day 38, "Forgiveness."

### Day 34  Heavenly Helpers

1. Cathy Taylor with Nancy Aguilar, *Guideposts*, "Healed by Heavenly
Angels: A Woman Battling Cancer Is Visited by Angels," accessed December 4, 2023, https://guideposts.org/angels-and-miracles/angels/healed-by
-heavenly-angels.

### Day 37  Healthy Soul

1. Clemson University Cooperative Extension Service, "Stress Management for the Health of It," National Ag Safety Database, accessed
December 4, 2023, https://nasdonline.org/1445/d001245/stress-manage
ment-for-the-health-of-it.html; Smitha Bhandari, "The Effects of Stress
on Your Body," December 8, 2021, https://www.webmd.com/balance/stress
-management/effects-of-stress-on-your-body.

### Day 38  Forgiveness

1. "Woman's Miraculous Healing Comes from Radical Forgiveness," *The
700 Club* YouTube channel, August 23, 2018, https://youtu.be/OFPGIaYI6ZI.

### Day 40  Body Wise

1. University of North Carolina at Chapel Hill, "Only 12 Percent
of American Adults Are Metabolically Healthy, Study Finds," Science

Daily, November 28, 2018, https://www.sciencedaily.com/releases/2018/11/181128115045.htm.

2. Anahad O'Connor, "What Are Ultra-Processed Foods? What Should I Eat Instead?," *Washington Post*, September 27, 2022, https://www.washingtonpost.com/wellness/2022/09/27/ultraprocessed-foods.

For the past 25 years, **Steve Austin** has been ministering to the sick—first as a volunteer, then as a pastor—in the largest medical center in the world—the Texas Medical Center in Houston, Texas. In 2021, after completing chaplaincy training at MD Anderson Cancer Center, he launched Living Hope Chaplaincy, a 501(c)(3) nonprofit organization that puts teams of trained volunteers in hospitals to provide spiritual care to patients, patients' families, and health-care workers. His dream is to have teams in hospitals across America and internationally. You can visit the website at LivingHope Chaplaincy.org and follow Living Hope Chaplaincy on Facebook and Instagram.

Steve could not do what he does without the love and support of his amazing wife of almost 28 years, Suzie. They have two wonderful daughters, Lindsey and Lauren, and everybody's favorite family member—a sweet Maltipoo named Lulu. You can follow Steve on his personal Facebook page and in two Facebook groups he created: God Heals, where he shares encouragement for people battling sickness and where people can post their prayer requests; and Healthy You, which has daily health and wellness tips and recipes.

@SteveAustin111

@groups/874985123314528

@groups/realhealthyyou